Expect The
Unexpected

EXPECT THE UNEXPECTED

C.R.CRANE II

authorHOUSE®

AuthorHouse™
1663 Liberty Drive
Bloomington, IN 47403
www.authorhouse.com
Phone: 1-800-839-8640

First published by AuthorHouse   01/20/2012

ISBN: 978-1-4685-3789-5 (sc)
ISBN: 978-1-4685-3788-8 (hc)
ISBN: 978-1-4685-3787-1 (ebk)

Library of Congress Control Number: 2012901096

Printed in the United States of America

CONTENTS

ABOUT THE BOOK

Here within these pages lie a silver bullet between the eyes. A grim reminder clouds are only tombstones in the sky. In the graveyard of memories there are ghosts that still fly. Like vultures overhead waiting for dreams to die. Haunted by the questions that have no reply. Monuments with their stoney faces stand alone and cry. The Grim Reaper and Cupid in their coffin lie. Waiting to be resurrected by the readers who wonder why. I expect the unexpected to catch you by surprse.

ABOUT THE AUTHOR

C.R.CRANE II, born late 1958 Holden WV Logan County. The proud father of two sons Andrew Staton and Sean Vance. It's only out of love so strong I leave their legacy in poetry and song.

FOR TOM AND LISA
WITH LOVE

I DEDICATE THIS BOOK TO
NO ONE ELSE BUT YOU
THE READER WITH EYES
TO LOVE OR DESPISE
MY EVERY POINT OF VIEW

A LITTLE HAPPINESS AND SADNESS
A LITTLE TOUCH OF MADNESS
IF ONLY TO ENTERTAIN
SONGS TO MAKE YOU WONDER
WHAT SPELL AM I UNDER
WHAT HIDES INSIDE MY BRAIN
A WAR OF WORDS THAT RAGES
MEMORIES SPILLED UPON THE PAGES
PIECES OF MY LIFE EXPLAINED

C.R.C.II

THE TALK OF THE TOWN

MY FRIENDS ALL THINK I'M CRAZY
MY NEIGHBORS ALL THINK I DRINK
MY FAMILY TRIED TO SAVE ME
BY SENDING ME TO A SHRINK

THE DOCTOR SAID IT'S IN MY HEAD
AND MY HEART MUST BE CURSED
THERE'S NO CURE FOR THE WALKING DEAD
IT MUST BE LOVE OR SOMETHING WORSE

I'M IN LOVE WITH A SUMO WRESTLER
SHE LIKES TO THROW ME DOWN
MAKE NO MISTAKE I'M FLATTER THAN A PANCAKE
I ONLY WEIGH A HUNDRED POUNDS
I'M IN LOVE WITH A SUMO WRESTLER
SHE'S THE TALK OF THE TOWN

I GIVE HER KISSES AND ROMANCE
SHE LIKES WINE AND CANDLELIGHT
THE ROOM SPINS WHEN WE DANCE
SHE LIKES TO SQUEEZE ME TIGHT

SHE SAYS I KNOW THAT I'M BIG
BUT AINT THAT THE BEST PART
I'LL BREAK YOU LIKE A TWIG
IF YOU EVER BREAK MY HEART
I'M IN LOVE WITH A SUMO WRESTLER
SHE LIKES TO THROW ME DOWN

MAKE NO MISTAKE I'M FLATTER THAN A PANCAKE
I ONLY WEIGH A HUNDRED POUNDS
I'M IN LOVE WITH A SUMO WRESTLER
SHE'S THE TALK OF THE TOWN

WHEN MY BODY BOUNCES OFF THE FLOOR
I KNOW WHAT SHE'S THINKING OF
MY NEIGHBORS SAY IT SOUNDS LIKE WAR
WHEN THEY HEAR US MAKING LOVE

THE WINDOWS RATTLE ON THE RANCH
PICTURES ON THE WALL TAKE FLIGHT
THE DOORS DON'T STAND A CHANCE
THE ROOF FLYS OUT OF SIGHT

I'M IN LOVE WITH A SUMO WRESTLER
SHE LIKES TO THROW ME DOWN
MAKE NO MISTAKE I'M FLATTER THAN A PANCAKE
I'M HER STOMPING GROUND
I'M IN LOVE WITH A SUMO WRESTLER
SHE'S THE TALK OF THE TOWN

NOTE# UPBEAT COUNTRY TUNE/TOBY KEITH STYLE SONG/SILLY
AS IT MAY BE

DADDY WENT TO JAIL

WE WERE DRINKING BEER ON A SATURDAY NIGHT
HAVING FUN IN A ONE HORSE TOWN
DADDY WAS HOLDING MAMA TIGHT
AS THEY DANCED ROUND AND ROUND

A STRANGER WALKED BY WITH EVIL EYES
I TRIED TO LOOK BUT I COULDN'T
THE TROUBLE BEGAN FOR THAT EVIL MAN
WHEN HE TOUCHED MAMA WHERE HE SHOULDN'T

MAMA CLAWED HIS EYES OUT
DADDY RUNG HIS BELL
THERE WAS NEVER ANY DOUBT
HE WAS DEAD BEFORE HE FELL
MAMA RAN TO THE COURTHOUSE
DADDY WENT TO JAIL

I WAS YOUNG AND FULL OF LIFE
SO SURPRISED AT WHAT I SAW
THE STRANGER TRIED TO PULL HIS KNIFE
DADDY WAS FASTER ON THE DRAW

I REMEMBER THAT OLD GUNSLINGER
BEFORE HE BUCKLED TO HIS DEMISE
DADDY GAVE HIM THE MIDDLE FINGER
AND FIVE KNUCKLES BETWEEN THE EYES
MAMA PULLED HIS HAIR OUT
DADDY RUNG HIS BELL

THERE WAS NEVER ANY DOUBT
HE WAS DEAD BEFORE HE FELL
MAMA RAN TO THE COURTHOUSE
DADDY WENT TO JAIL

AFTER FIVE LONG YEARS AND GOOD BEHAVIOR
THEY BROUGHT DADDY BACK TO TOWN
THE JURY FINALLY RULED IN HIS FAVOR
MAMA WAS JUMPING UP AND DOWN

THE GUARD WALKED BY WITH STUPID EYES
I TRIED TO LOOK BUT I COULDN'T
THE TROUBLE BEGAN FOR THAT STUPID MAN
WHEN HE SAID SOMETHING THAT HE SHOULDN'T

MAMA KNOCKED HIS TEETH OUT
DADDY RUNG HIS BELL
THERE WAS NEVER ANY DOUBT
HE WAS DEAD BEFORE HE FELL
MAMA RAN FROM THE COURTHOUSE
DADDY WENT TO JAIL

NOTE# LISTENING TO WAYLON JENNINGS WHEN I WROTE THIS
ONE

RABBIT IN THE WOOD

THE LAST TIME I SAW HER
SHE WAS RUNNING IN THE RAIN
THE LAST THING SHE TOLD ME
SHE THOUGHT I WAS INSANE

I DIDN'T KNOW WHAT SHE MEANT
WHEN SHE SAID SHE DIDN'T CARE
WROTE A LETTER I NEVER SENT
SOMEBODY SAID SHE WASN'T THERE

SHE'S GONE GONE GONE
 SHE'S GONE FOR GOOD
SHE'S GONE GONE GONE
LIKE A RABBIT IN THE WOODS

I DIDN'T KNOW I LOVED HER
UNTIL LONELINESS FILLED ME WITH DISPAIR
NOW I WOULD LIKE TO HUG HER
LIKE A BIG OLD GRIZZLY BEAR

MY LOVE GUN IS FULLY LOADED
AND I KEEP MY POWDER DRY
I AM HUNTING DAY AND NIGHT
WITH TEARS I CAN'T DISQUISE

SHE'S GONE GONE GONE
SHE'S GONE FOR GOOD
SHE'S GONE GONE GONE
LIKE A RABBIT IN THE WOODS

I'M LOSING POUNDS BY LEAPS AND BOUNDS
I'M SKINNY AS A RAIL
THERE'S A TOMBSTONE ON SACRED GROUND
IT SAYS WELCOME TO THE BUNNY TRAIL
LAST NIGHT I THOUGHT I SAW HER
SHE WAS RUNNING THROUGH MY MEMORIES
I GRABBED MY GUN FULL OF FUN
BUT ALL I SHOT WERE TREES

SHE' GONE GONE GONE
SHE'S GONE FOR GOOD
SHE'S GONE GONE GONE
LIKE A RABBIT IN THE WOODS

NOTE# UPBEAT SILLY COUNTRY SONG/MISTER CRANE IS QUITE
INSANE HA HA

SUZI MY LOVE

SITTING HERE IN MY ROCKING CHAIR
REMEMBERING ALL THOSE SUMMER DAYS
MY HEART PROVED THAT IT CARED
IN A THOUSAND DIFFERENT WAYS

MY HAND WROTE YOU SILLY POEMS
AND A HUNDRED LOVE SONGS
SENT YOU FLOWERS BY THE DOZEN
AND LETTERS TEN PAGES LONG

I'M NOT TRYING TO .... EMBARASS YOU
YOU'RE IN MY HALL OF FAME
PLEASE DON'T YOU BE .... MAD AT ME
IF I SHOULD MENTION YOUR NAME
SUZI MY LOVE

I TOOK YOU TO THE MOVIES
AND ALL MY FAVORITE SPOTS
YOU KISSES COULD ALWAYS MOVE ME
MAKE MY BLOOD RUN HOT

I KNOW IT WAS YEARS AGO
WHEN YOU STARTED HAUNTING ME
THIS OLD SOUL STILL DOESN'T KNOW
WHY YOU STOPPED WANTING ME

I'M NOT TRYING TO .... EMBARASS YOU
WHEN I SING ABOUT OLD FLAMES
YOU'RE ON THE WALL ....WATCHING TEARDROPS FALL
PRETTY FACE IN A SILVER FRAME
SUZI MY LOVE

SITTING HERE IN MY ROCKING CHAIR
REMEMBERING ALL THOSE WINTER DAYS
SPRINGTIME WAS IN THE AIR
BEFORE WE WENT ALL THE WAY

NIGHTS FILLED WITH MUSIC AND LAUGHTER
AND CARS THAT GO FAST
MY NERVES DIDN'T WRECK UNTIL AFTER
YOU PUT ME IN YOUR PAST
IF I SHOULD MENTION YOUR NAME SUZI MY LOVE

I'M NOT TRYING TO .... EMBARASS YOU
YOU'RE IN MY HALL OF FAME
PLEASE DON'T YOU BE .... MAD AT ME

NOTE# THINK OF GLORY DAYS THAT FADE AWAY INTO A COUNTRY
BALLAD

BIG MOUTH BABY

DON'T PLAY ME FOR A FOOL
OR A SUCKER ON YOUR LINE
WITH LIPS SO MEAN AND CRUEL
DON'T PUCKER THEM NEXT TO MINE

I KNOW LOVE IS NEVER SIMPLE
IT GETS HARDER EVERY DAY
WHEN IT BECOMES A GIANT PIMPLE
THERE'S ONLY ONE THING TO SAY

SHUT YOUR BIG MOUTH BABY
DON'T YOU SAY A WORD
EVERYTHING YOU SAY NOW
I'VE ALREADY HEARD
YOU'RE A BIG CAT WITH CLAWS
I'M JUST A LITTLE BIRD
OH OH OH I WILL GO

YOU KNOW YOU USE TO THRILL ME
EVERY NIGHT AND EVERY DAY
BUT NOW YOU WANT TO KILL ME
WITH ALL YOUR CHEATING WAYS

BEFORE YOUR LIPS STARTED LIEING
I KNEW ALL THE FACTS
BEFORE MY EYES STARTED CRYING
I ALWAYS TOOK YOU BACK
SHUT YOUR BIG MOUTH BABY

DON'T YOU SAY A WORD
EVERYTHING YOU TELL ME NOW
I'VE ALREADY HEARD
YOU'RE A BIG CAT WITH CLAWS
I'M JUST A LITTLE BIRD
OH OH OH MY HEART GOES
ONCE I WAS YOUR PRISONER
YOUR KISSES HELD THE KEY
NOW I'VE DONE MY TIME
THE TRUTH SETS ME FREE

I'M LEAVING YOU YOUR GILDED CAGE
AND LOVERS YOU HAVE KNOWN
YOUR FACE MADE THE FRONT PAGE
YOUR COVER HAS BEEN BLOWN

SHUT YOUR BIG MOUTH BABY
DON'T YOU SAY A WORD
EVERYTHING YOU TELL ME NOW
I'VE ALREADY HEARD
YOU'RE A BIG CAT WITH CLAWS
I'M JUST A LITTLE BIRD
OHOHOH HERE I GO

NOTE# UPBEAT CONTEMPORARY KIND OF COUNTRY SONG/
SOFT ROCK MAYBE?

HERE COMES ME

OH NICK WITH SHOVEL AND PICK
HE WAS WORKING IN THE MINES
ONE DAY HE FLICKED HIS BIC
AND BLEW OFF HIS FAT BEHIND

PIECES WENT FLYING LIKE A ROCKET
THEY LANDED UP IN THE TREES
NICK HAD FLASHLIGHTS IN HIS POCKET
BUT HE FORGOT THE BATTERIES

HERE COMES ME AND MY FAMILY
WE ARE A CRAZY BUNCH
YOU BETTER NOT STEAL OUR WEED
OR TRY TO EAT OUR LUNCH
WE MIGHT BREAK YOUR KNEES
AND LAUGH WHILE THEY CRUNCH
WHEN GUYS GIVE THEIR WIVES MONEY
HERE COMES ME

OH STEVIE BOY GOT HIMSELF EMPLOYED
BUT HE HATED WORKING ON CARS
ROCK MUSIC WAS WHAT HE ENJOYED
STEVIE GOT FIRED FOR PLAYING GUITAR

HE'S PROUD OF HIS IRISH NAME
AND YES HIS HAIR IS RED
HE WOULD RATHER PLAY VIDEO GAMES
OR STAY ALL DAY IN BED

HERE COMES ME AND MY FAMILY

WE ARE A CRAZY BUNCH

YOU BETTER NOT STEAL OUR WEED

OR TRY TO EAT OUR LUNCH

WE MIGHT BREAK YOUR KNEES

AND LAUGH WHILE THEY CRUNCH

WHEN GUYS LEAVE THEIR WIVES LONELY

HERE COMES ME

OH NICOLE WAS A HAPPY SOUL

UNTIL THAT MAN CAME ALONG

NOW SHE STARES THROUGH DOUGHNUT HOLES

AND SINGS JOHNNY CASH SONGS

WE DON'T MIND SHE'S HALF BLIND

WE TOOK THE KEYS AWAY

BECAUSE SHE LIKES TO DRIVE SOMETIMES

THROUGH A BALE OF HAY

HERE COMES ME AND MY FAMILY

WE ARE A CRAZY BUNCH

YOU BETTER NOT STEAL OUR WEED

OR TRY TO EAT OUR LUNCH

WE MIGHT BREAK YOUR KNEES

AND LAUGH WHILE THEY CRUNCH

WHEN GUYS TREAT THEIR WIVES INDIFFERANTLY

HERE COMES ME

NOTE# UPBEAT COUNTRY TUNE/IS THIS CRAZY OR NOT?

JOHNNY BE BAD

WAY DOWN IN LOGAN TOWN
THE GIRLS GATHERED AFTER SCHOOL
ALL THE GUYS STOOD AROUND
LIKE A BUNCH OF LOVESICK FOOLS

JOHNNY WAS LOOKING FOR HONEY
SOMEONE SWEET TO SHARE HIS WORLD
SANDY SAID IT MAY SOUND FUNNY
BUT I'M NOT THAT KIND OF GIRL

I WON'T PRETEND I LOVE YOU
I'M NO ANGEL IN WHITE
ALL I'LL EVER ASK OF YOU
JOHNNY BE BAD TONIGHT
TONIGHT
JOHNNY BE BAD TONIGHT

HE WAS DRESSED FOR SUCCESS
LIKE A COWBOY ON THE PROWL
SHE WAS QUICK WITH HER LIPS
LIKE BULLETS AT THE O.K. CORRAL

WORDS FLEW FROM HER HEART
WORDS FLEW FROM HER HEAD
THEY BLEW HIS RELIGION APART
WHEN HE HEARD WHAT SHE SAID

I WON'T PRETEND I LOVE YOU
I'M NO GOOD IN DAYLIGHT
ALL I'LL EVER ASK OF YOU
JOHNNY BE BAD TONIGHT
TONIGHT
JOHNNY BE BAD TONIGHT

SANDY BROKE DOWN HIS GUARD
BY WHISPERING IN HIS EAR
MAKING LOVE IS NEVER HARD
IF YOUR CONSCIENCE IS CLEAR
DARK CURTAINS COVERED THE WINDOWS
AT THE BLUEBIRD MOTEL
SOMEONE TURNED UP THEIR RADIO
WHEN THEY HEARD HER YELL

JOHNNY PLEASE PRETEND YOU LOVE ME
AND EVERYTHING'S ALL RIGHT
JOHNNY PLEASE THINK GOOD OF ME
JOHNNY BE BAD TONIGHT
TONIGHT
JOHNNY BE BAD TONIGHT

NOTE# A SPIN OFF OF CHUCK BERRY'S JOHNNY BE GOODE
CLASSIC WITH A CONTEMPORARY COUNTRY TWIST /FEMALE
VOCALS

SOMEBODY BETTER CALL

THE MAD SCIENTIST IS IN MY HEAD
LAUGHING AT ALL THE PAIN
I LET THAT WOMAN IN MY BED
FOR REASONS THAT I CAN'T EXPLAIN
I THINK I'M BETTER OFF DEAD
BECAUSE HER LOVE NO LONGER REMAINS

SOMEBODY BETTER CALL THAT WOMAN
TELL HER TO GET HERE QUICK
SOMEBODY BETTER CALL HER NUMBER
BECAUSE THIS MAN IS GETTING SICK
TELL HER THAT I'M DIEING
ONE MORE KISS MIGHT DO THE TRICK

I'0 LIKE TO TAKE MY WEED SICKLE
AND CUT OUT BOTH MY EYES
BEFORE I DROWN IN TEARS THAT TRICKLE
DOWN THE FACE THAT ALWAYS CRIES
NOW I'M SURE MY LIVER IS PICKLED
FROM TOO MUCH WHISKEY AND RYE

SOMEBODY BETTER CALL THE BARTENDER
TELL HIM TO GET HERE QUICK
SOMEBODY BETTER CALL HIS NUMBER
BECAUSE THIS MAN IS GETTING SICK
TELL HIM THAT I'M DIEING
ONE MORE DRINK MIGHT DO THE TRICK

THAT GYPSY CAME AND STOLE MY BRAIN
SHE LEFT A NOTE THAT SAID
SOMETIMES LOVE IS A BALL AND CHAIN
THAT DRAGS YOU DOWN IN BED
BUT HER NOTE NEVER DID EXPLAIN
WHY SHE LEFT ME HERE FOR DEAD
SOMEBODY BETTER CALL THE DOCTOR
TELL HIM TO GET HERE QUICK
SOMEBODY BETTER CALL HIS NUMBER
BECAUSE THIS MAN IS GETTING SICK
TELL HIM THAT I'M DIEING
AND MY BROKEN HEART NEEDS FIXED
SOMEBODY BETTER NOT CALL AT ALL
BECAUSE MY BUCKET JUST GOT KICKED

NOTE# KIND OF A PHONE RINGING DING A LING CONTEMPORARY
COUNTRY TUNE

BIG BEN

ONE EYED CHARLIE WAS LOOKING KNARLY
WHEN HE RODE INTO LOGAN TOWN
HE JUMPED OFF THAT OLD HARLEY
HIS ONE EYE WAS LOOKING AROUND

HE ASKED US HAVE WE SEEN HIM
A BIG MAN DRESSED IN BLACK
THERE'S NO MAYBE HE'S GOT MY BABY
NOW I WANT MY BABY BACK

WE SAID ....
YOU DON'T JUDGE A BOOK BY ITS' COVER
YOU DON'T PICK ON A FRIEND
YOU DON'T FOOL WITH ANOTHER MAN'S LOVER
AND YOU DON'T BOTHER BIG BEN

IT WAS ON A SATURDAY NIGHT
AT THE LOCAL BAR AND GRILL
GAMBLERS KNEW THE ODDS WERE RIGHT
THEY BET CHARLIE WOULD BE KILLED

WHEN CHARLIE WALKED THROUGH THE DOORWAY
NOT A SINGLE SOUL LAUGHED
BIG BEN STOOD LIKE A GIANT REDWOOD
AND HE BLOCKED CHARLIES' PATH

WE SAID ...

YOU DON'T JUDGE A BOOK BY ITS' COVER

YOU DON'T PICK ON A FRIEND

YOU DON'T FOOL WITH ANOTHER MANS' LOVER

AND YOU DON'T BOTHER BIG BEN

CHARLIE WAS SMALL ONLY FIVE FEET TALL

BUT HE HAD A BIG GUN

BIG BEN SAID CHARLIE YOU ARE DEAD

IF YOUR LITTLE LEGS DON'T RUN

THE VOICE OF DOOM ECHOED THROUGH THE ROOM

FIRE FLEW FROM THAT FORTYFOUR

YOU COULD HEAR THE CROWD SCREAM OUT LOUD

BIG BEN ISN'T BIG ANYMORE

WE SAID ....

YOU DON'T JUDGE A BOOK BY ITS' COVER

YOU DON'T KIDNAP A NEW HARLEY

YOU DON'T FOOL WITH ANOTHER MANS' LOVER

AND YOU DON'T STEAL FROM CHARLIE

NOTE# KIND OF A SPIN OFF TRIBUTE TO JIM CROCE'S-YOU DON'T
MESS AROUND WITH JIM

I KNEW A LONELY MAN

I KNEW A LONELY MAN
IN THE TWILIGHT OF HIS LIFE
HE SAID DO THE BEST YOU CAN
TAKE CARE OF YOUR KIDS AND WIFE

HE BUMMED MY LAST CIGARETTE
AND ASKED ME FOR A LIGHT
HE SAID DON'T YOU EVER FORGET
YOUR FAMILY NEEDS YOU HOME AT NIGHT

HE SAID I MADE A MISTAKE
ONE THAT I CAN'T WITHDRAW
EXCEPT FOR THIS ENDLESS HEARTACHE
BOY I LOST IT ALL
I WASN'T THERE FOR HER
 WHEN HEAVEN CALLED

HE SAID THAT HE WAS WORKING
TRYING TO MAKE ENDS MEET
SOMETIMES TWELVE HOURS A DAY
AND SEVEN DAYS A WEEK

HE SAID HE WAS TOO BUSY
HE DIDN'T SEE THE SIGNS
SHE ALWAYS HAD A BRAVE FACE
THAT THE PAIN HID BEHIND

HE SAID I MADE A MISTAKE
ONE THAT I CAN'T WITHDRAW
EXCEPT FOR THIS ENDLESS HEARTACHE
BOY I LOST IT ALL
I WASN'T THERE FOR HER
WHEN HEAVEN CALLED

I KNEW A LONELY MAN
IN THE FINAL DAYS OF HIS LIFE
I SAID I'M DOING THE BEST I CAN
TAKING CARE OF MY KIDS AND WIFE

I BUMMED HIS LAST CIGARETTE
AND ASKED HIM FOR A LIGHT
I TOLD HIM I WILL NEVER FORGET
MY FAMILY NEEDS ME HOME AT NIGHT

I SAID YOU MADE A MISTAKE
ONE THAT YOU CAN'T WITHDRAW
EXCEPT FOR THE ENDLESS HEARTACHE
MISTER YOU LOST IT ALL
I WAS THERE FOR HIM
WHEN HEAVEN CALLED
I WAS THERE FOR HIM
WHEN HEAVEN CALLED

NOTE# KIND OF A SLOW BLUESY SAD COUNTRY SONG/TEAR
JERKER?

SHE'S GOT IT ALL

SHE'S GOT A RING ON HER FINGER
A BRAND NEW HOUSE AND CAR
SHE ALWAYS WANTED TO BE A SINGER
NOW SHE'S MY FAVORITE SUPERSTAR

IT'S PLAIN TO SEE SHE'S DONE WITH ME
SHE'S ON STAGE WHERE SHE BELONGS
I THREW A ROCK THROUGH MY T.V.
BECAUSE SHE SANG OUR FAVORITE SONG

SHE'S GOT DIAMONDS BY THE DOZEN
A REMBRANDT HANGING ON HER WALL
SHE'S GOT MY LOVE AND MY ACHING HEART
SHE'S GOT IT ALL
MAN SHE'S GOT IT ALL

SHE'S GOT HERSELF A RICH OLD MAN
AND A BRAND NEW ATTITUDE
WHILE CHASING DREAMS AND MAKING PLANS
SHE FORGOT ABOUT THIS DUDE

I'M SITTING HERE DROWNING IN MY BEER
I BET SHE'S SWIMMING IN CHAMPAGNE
FOR HER THE SKIES ARE ALWAYS CLEAR
BUT ALL I GET IS RAIN

SHE'S GOT CREDIT CARDS BY THE HANDFUL

SHE'S GOT FANS IN MONTREAL

SHE'S GOT MY LOVE AND MY ACHING HEART

SHE'S GOT IT ALL

MAN SHE'S GOT IT ALL

I GOT DIRTY DISHES IN THE SINK

SHE'S GOT A BUTLER AND A MAID

I GOT SOMETHING ON MY BOOTS THAT STINK

BILLS IN THE MAIL I NEVER PAID

IF I SHOULD CONFESS ABOUT THIS MESS

I KNOW THAT I'M TO BLAME

WHILE SHE WORKED HARD FOR SUCCESS

MY LAZY WAYS REMAINED THE SAME

SHE'S GOT MONEY BY THE MILLIONS

LOVERS AT HER BECK AND CALL

SHE'S GOT MY LOVE AND MY ACHING HEART

SHE'S GOT IT ALL

MAN SHE'S GOT IT ALL

NOTE# CONTEMPORARY COUNTRY/ALAN JACKSON?

MY BEAUTIFUL
HILLBILLY BAND

I GOT PATTY ON THE PIANO
RIGHT HERE IN LOGAN TOWN
I GOT BETTY ON THE BANJO
I LOVE THAT COUNTRY SOUND

I GOT DREAMA ON THE DRUMS
AND MELINDA ON THE BASS
SUZI MAKES HER GUITAR WEEP
WHEN SHE SINGS AMAZING GRACE

I GOT MYSELF FIVE COUNTRY GIRLS
WHO ARE ALWAYS IN DEMAND
IN PIGTAILS AND LONG BLOND CURLS
PLEASE GIVE THEM A HAND
WEARING RHINESTONES AND IMITATION PEARLS
MY BEAUTIFUL HILLBILLY BAND

THEY GOT THE OLD MEN DREAMING
ALL ABOUT THEIR YOUNGER DAYS
THEY GOT THE OLD WOMEN SCREAMING
BEGGING THEM TO GO AWAY

BECAUSE WHEN THEIR MEN GET HOME
AND OUT GOES THE LIGHT
THEIR HUSBANDS' HANDS LIKE TO ROAM
AND KEEP THEM UP ALL NIGHT

I GOT MYSELF FIVE COUNTRY GIRLS

WHO ARE ALWAYS IN DEMAND
IN PIGTAILS AND LONG BLOND CURLS
PLEASE GIVE THEM A HAND
WEARING RHINESTONES AND IMITATION PEARLS
MY BEAUTIFUL HILLBILLY BAND

IN TIGHT JEANS AND SHORT DRESSES
THEY ALL LOOK SO GOOD
IN CHURCH THE PREACHER MAN CONFESSES
HIS WOODIE AINT MADE OF WOOD
THEY SING ABOUT LOVE AND MONEY
AND WHY GIRLS GET THE BLUES
I PAY THEM WITH MY KISSES
AND A BUNCH OF I.O.U.S

I GOT MYSELF FIVE COUNTRY GIRLS
WHO ARE ALWAYS IN DEMAND
IN PIGTAILS AND LONG BLOND CURLS
PLEASE DONATE WHAT YOU CAN
THEY DESERVE REAL DIAMONDS AND PEARLS
MY BEAUTIFUL HILLBILLY BAND
THERE'S NOTHING BETTER IN THIS WORLD
MY BEAUTIFUL HILLBILLY BAND

NOTE# COUNTRY HOEDOWN KIND OF SONG/THANKS TO ALL
THE LADIES

YOUR HEART WON'T PARDON ME

THERE'S NO RHYME OR REASON
FOR THE CHANGING OF THE SEASONS
I'M STILL HERE BEHIND THESE WALLS
IN THIS PLACE FULL OF SADNESS
THERE'S NO METHOD TO MY MADNESS
I'M STILL WAITING FOR YOUR CALL

FOR ALL MY CRIMES I'M DOING TIME
IN YOUR PRISON FULL OF MEMORIES
ALL THE GUARDS LOOK COLD AND HARD
IN THEIR HANDS THEY HOLD THE KEYS
THEY WON'T LET ME IN YOUR YARD
BECAUSE YOUR HEART WON'T PARDON ME
NO YOUR HEART WON'T PARDON ME

FORGIVE ME FOR HEAVENS' SAKE
I ONLY MADE A FEW MISTAKES
ONE WAS WITH PAPER AND PEN
I SHOULD HAVE KNOWN BETTER
THAN TO KEEP THAT LETTER
WRITTEN BY MY EXGIRLFRIEND

FOR THAT CRIME I SPEND MY TIME
WRAPPED IN CHAINS NO ONE SEES
ALL YOUR GUARDS LOOK COLD AND HARD
IN THIS JAIL FULL OF JEALOUSY
THEY KEEP ME BARRED FROM YOUR YARD

BECAUSE YOUR HEART WON'T PARDON ME
NO YOUR HEART WON'T PARDON ME

NOW LIFE HAS NO MEANING
SINCE YOU CONVICTED ME OF DREAMING
AND TALKING AGAINST MY WILL
BECAUSE OF ALL YOUR DOUBTS
I'M GUILTY OF STEPPING OUT
WITH A GIRL WHO WAS NEVER REAL

FOR THAT CRIME I PAY EVERY
TIME WHEN I DREAM OF BEING
FREE ALL YOUR GUARDS LAY DOWN THEIR CARDS
AND THEY COME RUNNING AFTER ME
THEY DRAG ME BACK ACROSS YOUR YARD
KICKING AND SCREAMING IN AGONY
BECAUSE YOUR HEART WON'T PARDON ME
NO YOUR HEART WON'T PARDON ME

NOTE# TRADITIONAL COUNTRY BALLAD

14

I LOVE THEM ALL

SOME PEOPLE CARE ABOUT WORLDLY AFFAIRS
AND THERE ARE PEOPLE WHO DON'T
LISTEN TO THIS SONG IF YOU DARE
I'LL TELL YOU SOMETHING THEY WON'T

I DON'T CARE ABOUT GIRLS' HAIR
OR IF THEY ALL GO BALD
I'LL RUN MY FINGERS THROUGH EMPTY AIR
AND RUB THEIR HEADS WITH ARMOURALL

EVERYBODY WANTS A LITTLE SOMETHING
FAT OR SKINNY-SHORT AND TALL
EVERYBODY NEEDS TO LOVE SOMEBODY
LORD KNOWS I LOVE THEM ALL I LOVE THEM ALL

I DON'T CARE WHAT THEY WEAR
BUSINESS SUITS OR BAGGY OLD CLOTHES
I'M NOT SURPRISED WHAT'S UNDER THERE
MY IMAGINATION ALREADY KNOWS

I SWEAR I'M GETTING MY SHARE
BECAUSE I NEVER DISCRIMINATE
AS LONG AS THEY SAY THEY CARE
MY HEART WILL NEVER BREAK

EVERYBODY WANTS A LITTLE SOMETHING
FAT OR SKINNY-SHORT AND TALL
EVERYBODY NEEDS TO LOVE SOMEBODY
LORD KNOWS I LOVE THEM ALL
I LOVE THEM ALL

IT'S FUNNY WHEN IT COMES TO MONEY
I DON'T CHARGE THEM A DIME
THEY CALL ME SWEETIE PIE AND HONEY
I CALL THEM ALL THE TIME
I DON'T CARE IF THEY GET WELFARE
I'M NOT THAT KIND OF MAN
AS LONG AS THE LOVE IS THERE
I'LL TAKE ALL THAT I CAN

EVERYBODY WANTS A LITTLE SOMETHING
FAT OR SKINNY-SHORT AND TALL
EVERYBODY NEEDS TO LOVE SOMEBODY
LORD KNOWS I LOVE THEM ALL I LOVE THEM ALL

NOTE# UPBEAT CONTEMPORARY COUNTRY SONG

15

I LOVE LONG GOODBYES

I KNOW YOU THINK YOU'RE FUNNY
WHEN ALL YOUR FRIENDS COME AROUND
DO YOU HEAR ME LAUGHING HONEY
WHEN MY HEART HITS THE GROUND

YOU TAKE MY LOVE FOR GRANTED
EVERY SINGLE DAY OF MY LIFE
ALL THE FLOWERS THAT I PLANTED
YOU CUT DOWN WITH A KNIFE

WHEN YOU BURN ME WITH YOUR LIES
AND YOUR LAUGHTER MAKES ME CHOKE
WHEN YOU DUD OUT MY BROWN EYES
I'M THE BUTT OF ALL YOUR JOKES
DARLING CAN YOU TELL ME WHY
I LOVE LONG GOODBYES

I BUILT YOU A NICE HOME
I BOUGHT YOU A NEW CAR
HALF THE TIME I SLEEP ALONE
AND DON'T KNOW WHERE YOU ARE

YOU PAWNED MY OLD LAWN MOWER
TO BUY A NEW HAIRDO
YOU SOLD MY OLD LEAF BLOWER
AND GAVE AWAY MY BOWLING SHOES

WHEN YOU KICK ME TO THE CURB
AND MY DREAMS GO UP IN SMOKE

WHEN YOU STEP ON THIS OLD TURD
I'M THE BUTT OF ALL YOUR JOKES
DARLING HERE COMES THE REASON WHY
I LOVE LONG GOODBYES

I KNOW YOUR LOVE IS PHONY
BUT SOMETHING MAKES ME STAY
IT'S THE THOUGHT OF PAYING ALIMONY
MAKES ME LOVE YOU ANYWAY
I KNOW YOU THINK YOU'RE FUNNY
WHEN ALL YOUR FRIENDS COME AROUND
DO YOU HEAR ME LAUGHING HONEY
EVERY TIME YOU PUT ME DOWN

WHEN YOU BURN ME WITH YOUR LIES
AND YOUR SMILE LEAVES ME BROKE
WHEN YOU DUD OUT MY BROWN EYES
I'M THE BUTT OF ALL YOUR JOKES
NOW YOU KNOW THE REASON WHY
I LOVE LONG GOODBYES
I LOVE LONG GOOD BYES

16

YOURS FOREVER MORE

LADY DO YOU EVER SIT AND LISTEN
WHEN THE NIGHT IS QUIET AND STILL
HAVE YOU EVER SEEN THE TEARS GLISTEN
IN THE EYES OF THE WHIPPORWILL

DARLING DO YOU REMEMBER ME AT ALL
WHEN YOU LIE AWAKE IN YOUR ROOM
HOW MANY SUMMER DAYS DO YOU RECALL
WHEN OUR LOVE WAS IN FULL BLOOM

ON THE WINGS OF DOVES I SEND MY LOVE
A LOVE I CAN'T IGNORE
ON A WHISPERING WIND THESE WORDS I SEND
STRAIGHT TO YOUR DOOR
ALL THOSE DOVES AND POEMS FILLED WITH LOVE
THEY ARE YOURS FOREVER MORE

SO YOU CAN SEE AND REMEMBER ME
EACH AND EVERY VALENTINES' DAY
OPEN THE BOOK AND TAKE A LOOK
READ WHAT I HAVE TO SAY

WHEN YOU WARM YOUR FEET BY THE FIRE
LET ME TELL YOU A TALE
A STORY ABOUT LOVE AND DESIRE
AND MY HEARTS' FINAL FAREWELL

ON THE WINGS OF DOVES I SEND MY LOVE
A LOVE I CAN'T IGNORE

ON A WHISPERING WIND THESE WORDS I SEND
STRAIGHT TO YOUR DOOR
ALL THOSE DOVES AND POEMS FILLED WITH LOVE
THEY ARE YOURS FOREVER MORE

LADY WILL YOU SAY THERE'S SOMETHING MISSING
NOW THAT YOU KNOW HOW I FEEL
COULD IT BE THE LIPS YOU AIN'T KISSING
AND THE MAN WHO LOVES YOU STILL

HOPE YOU KEEP THE CARDS AND LETTERS
AND EVERY PAGE OF MY POETRY
BUT IF YOU SHOULD FIND MY HEART
WILL YOU SEND IT BACK TO ME

ON THE WINGS OF DOVES I SEND MY LOVE
A LOVE I CAN'T IGNORE
ON A WHISPERING WIND THESE WORDS I SEND
STRAIGHT TO YOUR DOOR
ALL THOSE DOVES AND POEMS FILLED WITH LOVE
THEY ARE YOURS FOREVER MORE
I AM YOURS FOREVER MORE

NOTE# TRADITIONAL COUNTRY BALLAD

17

GUYS AND GIRLS

HEY GIRLS WHY DON'T YOU COME SEE ME
WE CAN GO FOR A SPIN
I WANT TO TALK ABOUT BEING LONELY
AND MY LAST BOYFRIEND

HE SAID THAT HE LOVED ME
AND I WAS ONE OF A KIND
BUT WHILE I WAS DREAMING OF HIM
HE WAS ROBBING MY MIND

I NEED SOMEBODY TO SHOW ME
WHY LOVE AIN'T FAIR
I NEED SOMEBODY TO TELL ME
WHY SHOULD I CARE
BUT WHAT I REALLY NEED TO KNOW IS
ARE THERE ANY NICE GUYS OUT THERE
ARE THERE ANY NICE GUYS OUT THERE

HE STOLE ALL MY SWEET KISSES
AND LEFT ME CRYING IN THE DARK
BECAUSE I WOULDN'T GRANT HIS WISHES
AND GIVE IN WHEN WE PARKED

I'M SURE YOU ALL KNOW HIM
SO I WON'T MENTION HIS NAME
I'M SURE I'LL OUTGROW HIM
BUT IT HURTS JUST THE SAME

I NEED SOMEBODY TO SHOW ME

WHY LOVE AIN'T FAIR
I NEED SOMEBODY TO TELL ME
WHY SHOULD I CARE
BUT WHAT I REALLY NEED TO KNOW IS
ARE THERE ANY NICE GUYS OUT THERE
ARE THERE ANY NICE GUYS OUT THERE

HEY GIRLS WHY DON'T YOU COME SEE ME
WE CAN GO FOR A SPIN
WE CAN TALK ABOUT THE BIRDS AND BEES
AND MY NEW BOYFRIEND

HE SAYS THAT HE LOVES ME
AND I'M ONE OF A KIND
BUT WHILE HE'S DREAMING OF ME
I'M ROBBING HIS MIND

HE NEEDS SOMEBODY TO SHOW HIM
WHY LOVE AINT FAIR
HE NEEDS SOMEBODY TO TELL HIM
WHY SHOULD HE CARE
BUT WHAT HE REALLY NEEDS TO KNOW IS
ARE THERE ANY NICE GIRLS OUT THERE
ARE THERE ANY NICE GIRLS OUT THERE

NOTE# TEEN/FEMALE POP SONG/ONE FOR THE LADIES

18

I'M ON FIRE

LOVE IS LIKE A ROLLER COASTER
FASTER THAN A FOURSPEED CAR
HOTTER THAN TOAST IN MY TOASTER
SWEETER THAN A CANDY BAR

HONEY WILL YOU STILL LOVE ME
WHEN THIS TIMEBOMB BLOWS
YOU CAN PUSH AND SHOVE ME
BUT I'LL NEVER LET GO

BECAUSE I'M ON FIRE
JUMPING THROUGH YOUR FLAMES
BURNING UP WITH DESIRE
CALLING OUT YOUR NAME
BABY YOU'RE A LIVE WIRE
LIGHTNING IN THE RAIN
BABY I'M ON FIRE
BUT I FEEL NO PAIN

HONEY WILL YOU STILL FEED ME
WHEN I'M OLD AND GREY
HONEY WILL YOU STILL NEED ME
WHEN MY ASHES BLOW AWAY

I'VE GOT MY JOHN WAYNE POSTER
HANGING RIGHT ABOVE MY BED
YOU GOT THIRTYEIGHTS IN YOUR HOLSTER
HANGING RIGHT BELOW YOUR HEAD

BABY I'M ON FIRE
JUMPING THROUGH YOUR FLAMES
BURNING UP WITH DESIRE
CALLING OUT YOUR NAME
BABY YOU'RE A LIVE WIRE
LIGHTNING IN THE RAIN
BABY I'M ON FIRE
BUT I FEEL NO PAIN

LOVE IS LI KE A ROLLER COASTER
FASTER THAN A FOURSPEED CAR
BURNING THE TOAST IN MY TOASTER
MELTING ALL MY CANDY BARS

HONEY WILL YOU STILL LOVE ME
WHEN THIS TIMEBOMB BLOWS
BEFORE YOU PUSH AND SHOVE ME
HOLD ON AND DON'T LET GO

BABY I'M ON FIRE
JUMPING THROUGH YOUR FLAMES
BURNING UP WITH DESIRE
CALLING OUT YOUR NAME
BABY YOU'RE A LIVE WIRE
LIGHTNING IN THE RAIN
BABY I'M ON FIRE
BUT I FEEL NO PAIN

NOTE# CLASSIC SOFT ROCK/POP SONG

19

LOVE

HEY THERE ALL YOU SQUARES
LONG TIME HIPPIES AND FOOLS
CUPID SAYS YOU BEST BEWARE
IDLE HANDS ARE THE DEVILS' TOOLS

SOME WILL STEAL WHAT THEY NEED
PENNIES FROM A DEAD MANS' EYES
BLINDED BY THEIR LONELINESS AND GREED
LOVE IS SOMETHING MONEY CAN'T BUY

LOVE LOVE LOVE
IN HONKY TONKS AND FANCY DIVES
LOVE LOVE LOVE
IT'S WHAT KEEPS THE WORLD ALIVE
LOVE LOVE LOVE
WE ALL NEED LOVE TO SURVIVE

HEY THERE WHO REALLY CARES
IF YOU FIND HAPPINESS AT ALL
BETTER HIDE THAT DOOBIE SOMEWHERE
BEFORE YOU GET HIGH AND FALL

YESTERDAYS' GHOSTS AND CHAINS THAT BIND
WON'T LET YOUR SPIRIT FLY
OPEN THE GRAVEYARD IN YOUR MIND
AND KILL THAT LONELY LULLABY

LOVE LOVE LOVE
IT'S A HARD BARGAIN YOU DRIVE

LOVE LOVE LOVE

PLEASE DON'T BURY MY HEART ALIVE

LOVE LOVE LOVE

WE ALL NEED LOVE TO SURVIVE

SOME WILL IGNORE THE TRUTH

SOME WILL SEE THE LIGHT

SOME WILL LOSE THEIR YOUTH

BUT NOT WITHOUT A FIGHT

THERE WON'T BE A HAPPY ENDING

IF WE LET HOPE DIE

I PRAY TO THE ANGELS NOW DESCENDING

FROM A CLEAR BLUE SKY

LOVE LOVE LOVE

FROM THE GRAVE I WILL ARISE

LOVE LOVE LOVE

I'LL CATCH THE DEVIL BY SURPRISE

LOVE LOVE LOVE

WE ALL NEED LOVE IN OUR LIVES

NOTE# ROCK/POP

20

HIGH ON RELIGION

I MET THE GIRL ON SUNDAY
I TRIED TO STEAL A KISS
I SAW THE GIRL ON MONDAY
I TRIED AGAIN BUT MISSED

SO I ASKED THE BROWNEYED GIRL
WHAT IS WRONG WITH ME
SHE SAID HERE IN MY WORLD
MY LIPS DON'T KISS EASILY

SHE SAID I GET HIGH ON RELIGION
GOSPEL MAKES ME ROCK AND ROLL
SHE SAID IF YOU WANT TO LOVE ME
TRUST IN GOD BECAUSE HE KNOWS
I GET HIGH ON RELIGION
GOSPEL MAKES ME ROCK AND ROLL

I FIRED UP A FAT JOINT
I OPENED UP A COLD BREW
SUDDENLY I SAW HER FINGER POINT
SHE SAID THE DEVIL'S AFTER YOU

I TURNED MY HEAD TO LOOK
BUT I SAW NO ONE THERE
I KNEW THEN I WAS HOOKED
ON THE FAIREST OF THE FAIR

SHE SAID I GET HIGH ON RELIGION
GOSPEL MAKES ME ROCK AND ROLL

SHE SAID IF YOU WANT TO LOVE ME
TRUST IN GOD BECAUSE HE KNOWS
I GET HIGH ON RELIGION
GOSPEL MAKES ME ROCK AND ROLL

I SPENT THE WEEK GOING CRAZY
WONDERING JUST WHAT I SHOULD DO
WENT OUT AND PICKED SOME DAISIES
BOUGHT A BOX OF CHOCOLATE TOO

I CALLED HER UP AND I CONFESSED
I WAS TIRED OF BEING COOL
SHE SAID WEAR YOUR VERY BEST
I'LL MEET YOU AT SUNDAY SCHOOL

NOW I'M GETTING HIGH ON RELIGION
GOSPEL MAKES ME ROCK AND ROLL
SHE'S GETTING ALL OF MY LOVE
GOD BLESS HER LOVELY SOUL
I'M GETTING HIGH ON RELIGION
GOSPEL MAKES ME ROCK AND ROLL

NOTE# UPBEAT CONTEMPORARY COUNTRY SONG

21

YOU DON'T NEED ME

EDGAR ALLEN SAW IT ALL
WHEN HE LIVED HERE BEFORE
I HEARD THE RAVEN CALL
WHEN YOU WALKED OUT THE DOOR
IN A HOUSE ABOUT TO FALL
I STILL MISS MY SWEET LENORE

HERE IN MY HEART OF HEARTS
LIKE A CASTLE OH SO GRAND
NOW OLD AND FALLING ALL APART
BECAUSE IT DOESN'T UNDERSTAND
WHY YOU DON'T NEED ME . . . .
TO BE YOUR MAN
YOU DON'T NEED ME

THERE'S A DREAM IN EVERY CORNER
HAUNTED BY YOUR PRETTY FACE
YOUR MEMORY KEEPS STABBING ME
IN THIS COLD AND LONELY PLACE
EVERY TEARDROP IS FILLED WITH SADNESS
BUT CRYING IS JUST A WASTE

HERE IN MY HEART OF HEARTS
LIKE A CASTLE IN QUICK SAND
HERE IS WHERE THE DIEING STARTS
CASTING SHADOWS ON THE LAND
BECAUSE YOU DON'T NEED ME . . . .
TO BE YOUR MAN
YOU DON'T NEED ME

MAD SCIENCETIST PUTS ME BACK TOGETHER
WITH RUSTY NAILS AND TWINE
NOW I LOVE THE RAINY WEATHER
AND I LOOK LIKE FRANKENSTEIN
BUT I HATE THE FIRE OF DESIRE
THAT BURNS INSIDE MY MIND

HERE IN MY HEART OF HEARTS
HEAVEN AND HELL MAKE THEIR DEMANDS
VINCENT PRICE SITS IN THE DARK
WITH A NEEDLE IN BOTH HANDS
HE FILLS MY BRAIN WITH NOVACANE
BUT I STILL DON'T UNDERSTAND
WHY YOU DON'T NEED ME . . . .
TO BE YOUR MAN
YOU DON'T NEED ME

NOTE# OLD VINCENT PRICE MOVIE/EDGAR ALLEN POES' THE
RAVEN/THE BEATLES'-I WANT TO BE YOUR MAN/GO FIGURE/
CLASSIC SOFT ROCK/POP

22

IT'S SO LONG

THE SUN IS BURNING DOWN THE DAYLIGHT
OFF TO BED I FLY
SWEET KISSES IN THE HEAT OF THE NIGHT
FILLING ME FULL OF SURPRISE

MY MAN KNOWS HOW TO HOLD ME
WHEN HIS FINGERS FIND THEIR WAY
I LOVE IT WHEN HE MOLDS ME
TURNS MY BODY INTO CLAY

OH BABY YOU ARE MY PRICELESS TREASURE
YOU ARE MY FAVORITE SONG
IN MY HANDS IT'S HARD TO MEASURE
OUR LOVE IS SO LONG SO LONG
SO LONG YOUR LOVE IS SO LONG

FROM THE SKY FORBIDDEN FRUITS ARE FALLING
WILD HORSES PULL THE PLOW
LIKE A SNAKE MY MAN COMES CRAWLING
HE'S IN MY GARDEN NOW

SLIPPING AND SLIDING BETWEEN MY FENCES
SO HE CAN MAKE ME PAY
FOR THIS QUESTION IN A SENTENCE
WHO TAUGHT YOU TO KISS THAT WAY

BECAUSE EVERY KISS PROLONGS THE PLEASURE
LIKE A NEVER ENDING SONG
IN MY HANDS IT'S HARD TO MEASURE

YOUR LOVE IS SO LONG
SO LONG SO LONG
YOUR LOVE IS SO LONG

YOU SAY YOUR MIDDLE NAME IS LOVERBOY
AND YOU'RE A WORK OF ART
YOU'RE BETTER THAN ANY BEDROOM TOY
NO MORE SPARKS IN THE DARK

HOW DO YOU KEEP YOUR COMPOSURE BOY
HOW DO YOU KEEP CONTROL
WHILE I GO CRAZY WHEN YOU TOUCH ME
SO DEEP INSIDE MY SOUL

OH BABY YOU ARE MY PRICELESS TREASURE
YOU ARE MY FAVORITE SONG
IN MY HANDS IT'S HARD TO MEASURE
YOUR LOVE IS SO LONG
SO LONG SO LONG
BABY IT'S SO LONG

NOTE# ONE FOR THE LADIES/FEMALE VOCALS/RECORDED BUT
NOT INCLUDED ON THE TRAVELING HILLBILLY CD/REWRITE

23

SMART WITH YOUR HEART

I WENT TO SEE THE WISEMAN
SITTING HIGH UP ON THE HILL
I EXPLAINED MY ACHES AND PAINS
AND WHY I MIGHT BE KILLED

I SAID I'M ALWAYS IN TROUBLE
WITH THE GIRLS AND THE LAW
TODAY A BABY'S ON THE WAY
HER DADDY AINT HAPPY AT ALL

THE WISEMAN CALLED ME A CHILD
HE SAID LISTEN TO ME SON
DON'T LET YOUR BIG HEAD
DO WHAT YOUR LITTLE HEAD DONE
ALWAYS BE SMART WITH YOUR HEART
PROTECT YOURSELF WHEN YOU HAVE FUN

I CLIMBED UP ON THAT ROCK
AND I LISTENED TO HIS ADVICE
HE SAID I'LL SURVIVE THE SHOCK
TRUE LOVE NEVER STRIKES TWICE

I JUMPED DOWN FROM HIS THRONE
LEAVING BEHIND THE BOY IN ME
THE WORDS WERE WRITTEN IN STONE
IT TAKES TWO TO MAKE THREE

THE WISEMAN CALLED ME A CHILD
HE SAID LISTEN TO ME SON

DON'T LET YOUR BIG HEAD
DO WHAT YOUR LITTLE HEAD DONE
ALWAYS BE SMART WITH YOUR HEART
PROTECT YOURSELF WHILE YOU ARE YOUNG

I WENT TO SEE HER DADDY
COLD SWEAT DRIPPING DOWN LIKE WATER
I EXPLAINED MY ACHES AND PAINS
AND WHY I LOVED HIS DAUGHTER
I SAID I'LL BE NO TROUBLE
MISTER PLEASE DON'T CALL THE LAW
BECAUSE TODAY MY LOVE WILL DOUBLE
PLEASE BE HAPPY FOR US ALL

HE CALLED ME A DIRTY NAME
AND SAID LISTEN TO ME SON
I SHOULD BUST YOUR BIG HEAD
FOR WHAT YOUR LITTLE HEAD DONE
IF YOU ARE SMART WITH YOUR HEART
I WON'T NEED MY OLD SHOTGUN
IF YOU ARE SMART WITH YOUR HEART
BE A MAN AND RAISE YOUR YOUNG

NOTE# KIND OF MIDTEMPO COUNTRY SONG/COULD BE A
BALLAD I GUESS/WHO KNOWS.

24

BYE BYE BLUE EYES

GIRL DON'T YOU TRY TO KISS ME
DON'T SAY THAT YOU WILL MISS ME
I KNOW YOUR LIPS LOVE TO LIE
AS YOU PACK YOUR BAGS TO LEAVE
YOU PACK AWAY THE AIR I BREATH
LEAVING ME WITH ONLY ONE REPLY

BYE BYE BLUE EYES
I'VE HEARD YOU LAUGH AND WATCHED YOU CRY
I'VE SEEN YOU LOOKING UP AT THE SKY
BYE BYE BLUE EYES
BLUE EYES GOODBYE

WHEN YOU SAY YOU NEED TO LIVE
DOES THAT MAKE IT EASIER TO FORGIVE
THE MISTAKES LOVE MAKES BEFORE IT DIES
YOU SAY YOU NEED YOUR OWN SPACE
HONEY IS THERE REALLY SUCH A PLACE
WHERE PEOPLE GO TO FILL THEIR EMPTY LIVES

BYE BYE BLUE EYES
I'VE HEARD YOU LAUGH AND WATCHED YOU CRY
I'VE SEEN YOU LOOKING UP AT THE SKY
BYE BYE BLUE EYES
BLUE EYES GOODBYE

NO MATTER WHAT I DO OR SAY
YOU SPREAD YOUR WINGS AND FLY AWAY
LEAVING ME JUST ANOTHER LONELY GUY
NO MATTER WHAT I SAY OR DO
MY HEART WILL NEVER STOP LOVING YOU
I BELIEVE THE MEMORIES ARE WHY

BYE BYE BLUE EYES
I'VE HEARD YOU LAUGH AND WATCHED YOU CRY
I'VE SEEN YOU LOOKING UP AT THE SKY
BYE BYE BLUE EYES
BLUE EYES GOODBYE

IF YOU SHOULD EVER CHANGE YOUR MIND
HONEY I WON'T BE HARD TO FIND
I'LL BE SOMEWHERE THINKING OF YOU AND I
IF YOU ARE EVER BACK IN TOWN
GIVE ME A CALL OR COME AROUND
MAYBE THEN I COULD END THIS LONESOME LULLABY

BYE BYE BLUE EYES
I HEARD YOU LAUGH AND I WATCHED YOU CRY
I SAW YOU SO HIGH YOU TOUCHED THE SKY
BYE BYE BLUE EYES
BLUE EYES GOODBYE
BYE BYE BLUE EYES
BLUE EYES GOODBYE

NOTE# REWRITE/TRADIONAL COUNTRY BALLAD

25

EAT IT WHILE IT'S HOT

I SAW HER THROUGH THE CAFE WINDOW
POURING COFFEE AND SLINGING HASH
I SAW STEAM COMING OUT OF HER JEANS
SHE WAS FOGGING UP THE GLASS

MY LIPS GOT STRUCK BY A PASSING TRUCK
WHILE I WAS KISSING MY HEART GOODBYE
IT WAS LOVE AT FIRST SIGHT AND I WANTED A BITE
ONE LITTLE TASTE OF HER PIE

SHE SAID MISTER I SEE YOU HAVE NO MONEY
SO HERE'S A LITTLE FOOD FOR THOUGHT
IF YOU GOT A MANSIZE HUNGER HONEY
YOU BETTER EAT IT WHILE IT'S HOT
BECAUSE I'VE BEEN TOLD IT'S NO GOOD COLD
SO YOU BETTER EAT IT WHILE IT'S HOT

I BROKE MY NOSE AND STUBBED MY TOE
WHEN SHE TURNED OUT THE LIGHTS
SHE SAID LOVE IS HAIRY AND SOMETIMES SCARY
HOW BIG IS YOUR APPETITE

I SAID IT'S SMALL ONLY TEN INCHES TALL
BUT A LEGEND IN ITS' TIME
SHE WAS OFF THE CLOCK WHEN THE FRONT DOOR LOCKED
SHE SAID YOUR PLACE OR MINE

SHE SAID MISTER I HAVE NO NEED FOR MONEY
AND I DON'T DO THIS A LOT
BUT IF YOU NEED SOME GOOD LOVING HONEY
YOU BETTER EAT IT WHILE IT'S HOT
BECAUSE I'VE BEEN TOLD IT'S NO GOOD COLD
SO YOU BETTER EAT IT WHILE IT'S HOT

WITH BOTH HER ARMS AND ALL HER CHARMS
SHE SERVED UP QUITE A SPREAD
WHILE MY FACE WAS STUCK IN HER POT LUCK
SHE BLEW ME OUT OF BED

I CLIMBED BACK IN WITH A TOOTHLESS GRIN
MY TONGUE WAS ON THE FLOOR
WHAT DID SHE EXPECT FROM A NERVOUS WRECK
I SAID I'LL HAVE SOME MORE

SHE SAID MISTER I SEE YOU HAVE NO MONEY
SO HERE'S A LITTLE FOOD FOR THOUGHT
IF YOU GOT A MANSIZE HUNGER HONEY
YOU BETTER EAT IT WHILE IT'S HOT
BECAUSE I'VE BEEN TOLD IT'S NEVER GOOD COLD
SO YOU BETTER EAT IT WHILE IT'S HOT

NOTE# MY WEIRD SENSE OF HUMOUR STRIKES AGAIN/ROCKABILLY
SILLY

26

LET THE MEMORIES BEGIN

I KNOW THE END IS COMING
ON A WARM SUMMER BREEZE
WHEN I'M DEAD AND GONE
WILL YOU STILL REMEMBER ME

BENEATH BLUE SKIES AND GOLDEN SUNSETS
AND RAINBOWS IN THE RAIN
TRUE COLORS OF LOVE WITHOUT REGRETS
WILL BE ALL THAT REMAIN

WHEN I DIE PLEASE DON'T CRY
SCATTER MY ASHES IN THE WIND
YOUR LOVE WAS WORTH A TRY
I WOULD DO IT ALL AGAIN
PLAY A SONG AND WAVE GOODBYE
AND LET THE MEMORIES BEGIN

TEENAGE DREAMS AND CHILDISH GAMES
AND THAT FIRST TENDER TOUCH
KISSES HOTTER THAN THE HOTTEST FLAMES
BORN TO BURN SO MUCH

NOW THAT I AM OLDER
DOWN TO MY LAST BREATH
MY BONES ARE GETTING COLDER
AND IT SCARES ME TO DEATH

WHEN I DIE PLEASE DON'T CRY
SCATTER MY ASHES IN THE WIND
YOUR LOVE WAS WORTH A TRY
I WOULD DO IT ALL AGAIN
PLAY A SONG AND WAVE GOODBYE
AND LET THE MEMORIES BEGIN

IF I MAKE IT TO FALL
AFTER ANOTHER SPRING HAS SPRUNG
IF YOU REMEMBER ME AT ALL
REMEMBER WHEN WE WERE YOUNG
BENEATH BLUE SKIES AND GOLDEN SUNSETS
AND RAINBOWS IN THE RAIN
TRUE COLORS OF LOVE WITHOUT REGRETS
WILL BE ALL THAT REMAIN

WHEN I DIE PLEASE DON'T CRY
SCATTER MY ASHES IN THE WIND
YOUR LOVE WAS WORTH A TRY
I WOULD DO IT ALL AGAIN
PLAY A SONG AND WAVE GOODBYE
AND LET THE MEMORIES BEGIN

NOTE# KIND OF TRADITIONAL COUNTRY SONG

27

CHUBBY MAN

CHUBBY MAN WHAT'S THAT IN YOUR GRUBBY HANDS
IS IT A PIZZA IN A GIANT PAN
CHUBBY MAN I DON'T THINK I'LL EVER UNDERSTAND

WHY YOU HAVE TO BLOW BEFORE YOU GO
YOU NEVER SAY
AN'T YOU SEE THE FUMES ARE KILLING ME
I'M BLOWN AWAY

CHUBBY MAN DON'T FORGET TO WASH YOUR HANDS
FOR ALL GODS' CREATURES THERE'S A PLAN
CHUBBY MAN I DON'T THINK I'LL EVER UNDERSTAND

WHY THOSE CHICKEN LEGS WITH YOUR EGGS
PORKCHOPS ON YOUR PLATE
I HAVE SEEN CORNBREAD AND BEANS
PUDDING ON YOUR CAKE

CHUBBY MAN ARE YOU HEADED FOR THE PROMISED LAND
WITH A COLD PEPSI IN BOTH HANDS
CHUBBY MAN I'LL FIND THE ANSWER IF I CAN

WHY DON'T YOU HIDE THE BOMB INSIDE
BEFORE YOU SHATTER GLASS
THERE GOES YOUR CHAIR WITH YOUR UNDERWEAR
THANKSGIVINGS ARE A BLAST

OH CHUBBY MAN NOW I THINK I UNDERSTAND
YOU LOVE TURKEY WITH YOUR HAM

AND IT'S ALL BECAUSE
MAMA SPOILED YOU WITH HER OWN TWO HANDS
NOW YOU'RE LOOKING FOR A PLACE TO LAND
OH OH OH CHUBBY MAN

NOTE# PATTERNED AFTER ONE OF MY FAVORITE BEATLE
SONGS-(YESTERDAY)

28

JACK GOT CRAZY

HAVE YOU HEARD THAT OLD STORY
ONE ABOUT THAT BOY AND GIRL
A RHYME FOR ALL THE AGES
A STORY TOLD AROUND THE WORLD

WHAT HAPPENED TO ALL THEIR LOVE
WHERE DID IT FINALLY GO
WAS THERE A HAPPY ENDING
SOMEWHERE DOWN THE ROAD

JACK GOT CRAZY
JILL GOT QUICK
SHE FED HIM GRAVY
IT MADE JACK SICK
HE GRABBED HER DAISIES
SHE GRABBED HIS STICK
JACK GOT CRAZY
WHEN JILL SPLIT

WITH HIS HEART ON HER SHOULDER
SHE ROLLED IT DOWN THE HILL
IT SHATTERED LIKE A GLASS BOULDER
WHEN IT LANDED IN THE FIELD

SHE GATHERED UP HER LOVE HANDLES
AND CROWNED HIM WITH DISMAY
LEFT HIM JUMPING OVER LIGHTED CANDLES
BURNING HIS BUTT ALONG THE WAY

JACK GOT CRAZY

JILL GOT QUICK

SHE FED HIM GRAVY

IT MADE JACK SICK

HE STRANGLED HER DAISIES

SHE BROKE HIS STICK

JACK GOT CRAZY

WHEN JILL SPLIT

IF YOU ALL DON'T BELIEVE ME

JUST LOOK BACK IN THE WOODS

THERE GOES JACK AND THE BEANSTALK

WITH THE LITTLE RED RIDINGHOOD

IF YOU WANT TO KNOW THE ENDING

TO THE SILLY LOVE THEY HAD

JACK LOOKS LIKE A BOY LAUGHING

JILL LOOKS LIKE SHE'S REALLY MAD

JACK GOT CRAZY

JACK WAS QUICK

HE HID HER GRAVY

DOWN BY THE CRICK

HE'S FONDLING NEW DAISIES

SHE'S THROWING BIG BRICKS

JACK GOT CRAZY JILL GOT TRICKED

NOTE# DO I HAVE TO EXPLAIN WHAT INSPIRED THIS SILLY
COUNTRY SONG/UPBEAT

29

BORN TO PLAY

HE GREW UP LISTENING TO THE BEATLES
AND BECAME A ROLLING STONES FAN
WHEN HE BLEW HIS GUITAR INTO NEEDLES
BILLY JOINED A BRAND NEW BAND

ROCK AND ROLL OUT OF CONTROL
PARENTS POUNDING DOWN THE DOOR
PREACHER WANTS TO SAVE THEIR SOULS
BUT THEY DON'T HAVE ONE ANYMORE

BAD BOYS
OH THOSE BAD BOYS
ROCKING ALL NIGHT AND DAY
SOME CALL IT MUSIC
SOME CALL IT NOISE
P.T.A. WANTS TO PUT THEM AWAY
BAD BOYS
OH THOSE BAD BOYS
THEY WERE BORN TO PLAY

BREAKING OLD GROUND WITH A NEW SOUND
STEALING ALL THE YOUNG GIRLS 'HEARTS
LOVE AND HATE AND A TWIST OF FATE
TWO SONGS THAT TOP THE CHARTS

THEY GOT THE LITTLE GIRLS DREAMING
THEY GOT THE BOYS FEELING MEAN
THE GOT THE BIG GIRLS SCREAMING
BLOWING KISSES AT THEIR LIMOSINE

BAD BOYS

OH THOSE BAD BOYS

ROCKING ALL NIGHT AND DAY

SOME CALL IT MUSIC

SOME CALL IT NOISE

P.T.A. WANTS TO PUT THEM AWAY

BAD BOYS

OH THOSE BAD BOYS

THEY BORN TO PLAY

THEY GREW UP LISTENING TO OLD JOHNNY

WHEN JOHNNY WAS IN THE PEN

NOW THEY STASH AWAY THE CASH

ON A TRAIN ROLLING AROUND THE BEND

ROCK AND ROLL OUT OF CONTROL

SCHOOL BOOKS BURNING IN THE CORRIDOR

TEACHER SAYS I HOPE THEY GO

WHERE NO BAND HAS GONE BEFORE

BAD BOYS

OH THOSE BAD BOYS ROCKING ALL NIGHT AND DAY

SOME CALL IT MUSIC

SOME CALL IT NOISE

P.T.A. WANTS TO PUT THEM AWAY

BAD BOYS

OH THOSE BAD BOYS

THEY WERE BORN TO PLAY

HEY HEY HEY

THEY WERE BORN TO PLAY

NOTE# INSPIRED BY SPRINGSTEENS' BORN TO RUN/BORN IN THE U.S.A.

30

WHY SHE DIED

HAVE YOU COME TO GET MY BABY
ALONG WITH ALL MY FOOLISH PRIDE
IF YOU HAVEN'T SEEN HER LATELY
WHY DON'T YOU LOOK OUTSIDE

SHE'S SITTING THERE ON CINDERBLOCKS
LOOKING TIRED AND ALL ALONE
SHE'S MISSING ALL FOUR SHOCKS
AND A FEW PIECES OF CHROME

THE OIL BARONS KILLED HER
OH SO SLOWLY AT FIRST
SHE RAN UNTIL SHE WAS EMPTY
THAT'S WHEN HER MOTOR BURST
I COULDN'T AFFORD ALL HER DRINKING
THAT'S WHY .... SHE DIED .... OF THIRST
THAT'S WHY SHE DIED

I HAD TO SELL HER WHEELS
THE ONES THAT LOOKED SO COOL
TEXACO SAID I OWED A BILL
AND I WAS ACTING LIKE A FOOL

THE CASHIER HANDED ME THE TICKET
I THREW IT ON THE FLOOR
I TOLD THE MAN TO STICK IT
WHERE HE NEVER STUCK ANYTHING BEFORE

THE OIL BARONS KILLED HER

OH SO SLOWLY AT FIRST
SHE RAN UNTIL SHE WAS EMPTY
THAT'S WHEN HER MOTOR BURST
I COULDN'T AFFORD ALL HER DRINKING
THAT'S WHY .... SHE DIED .... OF THIRST THAT'S
WHY SHE DIED

WE HAD OUR SHARE OF GOOD TIMES
WE WOULD FLY DOWN THE ROAD
NOW HER BODY DOESN'T SHINE
AND HER TIRED EYES ARE CLOSED

TAKE IT EASY THERE MISTER TOW MAN
PLEASE BE GENTLE AS YOU GO
SHE'S MORE THAN JUST A TIN CAN
SHE'S A CLASSIC HEAD TO TOE

THE OIL BARONS KILLED HER
OH SO SLOWLY AT FIRST
SHE RAN UNTIL SHE WAS EMPTY
THAT'S WHEN HER MOTOR BURST
I COULDN'T AFFORD ALL HER DRINKING
THAT'S WHY .... SHE DIED .... OF THIRST
THAT'S WHY SHE DIED

NOTE# COUNTRY ANTHEM/BALLAD

31

LOVING BY THE POUND

FOREVER MEN HAVE DREAMED THE FISHERMAN'S DREAM
HOPING TO CATCH THE PERFECT TEN
AS FOR ME MY HEART DISAGREES
I DON'T LIKE MY WOMEN THIN

BECAUSE I'VE HAD PLENTY OF TALL AND SKINNY
WITH NO WEIGHT TO HOLD THEM DOWN
WHEN A LOT OF MEN AINT GETTING THEM ANY
I GET MY LOVING BY THE POUND
SHE'S THE BEST I EVER FOUND
YEAH I GET MY LOVING BY THE POUND

SHE'S A LITTLE CHUNKY AND KIND OF FUNKY
I LOVE TO WATCH HER RUN
SHE MAKES ME LAUGH AND TAKE NUDE PHOTOGRAPHS
I LOVE MY TON OF FUN

WHEN SHE GETS LAZY AND KIND OF CRAZY
I KNOW SHE'S IN THE DUMPS
THAT'S WHEN I SAY YOU LOOK GOOD TODAY
IN YOUR PANTYHOSE AND PUMPS

I'VE HAD PLENTY OF TALL AND SKINNY
TOO FRAGILE TO WRAP MY ARMS AROUND
WHEN ALL MY FRIENDS AINT GETTING ANY
I GET MY LOVING BY THE POUND
SHE'S THE BEST I EVER FOUND
YEAH I GET MY LOVING BY THE POUND

SHE LIKES TO SING AND BREAK MY SPRINGS
WHEN HER BODY BOUNCES INTO BED
I HOLD ON TIGHT WITH ALL MY MIGHT
COUNTING THE CURLERS ON HER HEAD

FOREVER MEN HAVE DREAMED THE COWBOY'S DREAM
IN HOPES OF ROPING THE WIND
AS FOR ME I SLEEP SO PEACEFULLY
WITH LOVE UP TO MY CHIN

I'VE HAD PLENTY OF TALL AND SKINNY
TINY TOOTHPICKS CAN'T HOLD ME DOWN
WHEN A LOT OF MEN AINT GETTING ANY
I GET MY LOVING BY THE POUND
SHE'S THE BEST I'VE EVER FOUND
YEAH I GET MY LOVING BY THE POUND

NOTE# KIND OF FUNKY CONTEMPORARY COUNTRY TUNE

32

PUPPY DOGS AND CHILDREN

DON'T STICK YOUR HEAD IN THE CLOUDS
AND SEARCH FOR REASONS TO BE UNKIND
DON'T YOU STAND TOO TALL OR PROUD
YOU MIGHT GROW OLD BEFORE YOUR TIME

DON'T GET GREEDY AND FORGET THE NEEDY
THEIR HOPE IS IN YOUR HANDS
FORGET THE RAT RACE AND LOOK ON A CHILD'S FACE
MAYBE THEN YOU WILL UNDERSTAND

PUPPY DOGS AND CHILDREN
SPREADING JOY FROM COAST TO COAST
PUPPY DOGS AND CHILDREN
IT'S THE SIMPLE THINGS THAT MEAN THE MOST
I LOVE MY PUPPY DOGS AND CHILDREN
AND THEY LOVE JELLY ON THEIR TOAST

YOU KNOW MATERIAL THINGS NEVER LAST
NO MATTER HOW MUCH THEY COST
IN YOUR LUST FOR A LITTLE GOLDDUST
YOU MIGHT FIND YOURSELF FOREVER LOST

DON'T TAKE YOUR LIFE FOR GRANTED
DON'T YOU COMMIT THAT SIN
BETTER RESURRECT THE DREAMS YOU PLANTED
AND LET THE SUNSHINE IN

PUPPY DOGS AND CHILDREN
SPREADING JOY FROM COAST TO COAST
PUPPY DOGS AND CHILDREN
IT'S THE SIMPLE THINGS THAT MEAN THE MOST
I LOVE MY PUPPY DOGS AND CHILDREN
AND THEY LOVE CASPER THE FRIENDLY GHOST

DON'T CLIMB OVER YOUR BEST FRIEND'S BACK
IN YOUR MAD RUSH FOR SUCCESS
HE MAY BE THE STRENGTH YOU LACK
WHEN YOUR LIFE BECOMES A MESS

BETTER WATCH THE BRIDGES THAT YOU BURN
ONCE YOU START IT'S HARD TO STOP
WHEN YOU REACH THE POINT OF NO RETURN
I HEAR IT'S LONELY AT THE TOP

PUPPY DOGS AND CHILDREN
SPREADING JOY FROM COAST TO COAST
PUPPY DOGS AND CHILDREN
IT'S THE SIMPLE THINGS THAT MEAN THE MOST
I LOVE MY PUPPY DOGS AND CHILDREN
AND THEY LOVE CATS AND MARSHMELLOW ROASTS

NOTE# TRADITIONAL COUNTRY BALLAD/REWRITE FROM MY
BOOK-THE EMPTY ROOM @AUTHORHOUSE.COM

33

SLEEP MY DARLING

YOU ARE MY FAITHFUL COMPANION
YOU ARE MY BEST FRIEND
WITH LOVE DEEPER THAN THE GRAND CANYON
YOUR LOVE HAS NO END

THAT'S WHY I ADORE YOU
THAT'S WHAT MAKES ME SAY
HONEY YOU ARE SO SPECIAL
IN OH SO MANY WAYS

I WON'T LET YOU COME TO HARM
WHEN WILLOW TREES BEGIN TO WEEP
I WILL HOLD YOU IN MY ARMS
SWEET DREAMS MY DARLING .... GO TO SLEEP

REST YOUR HEAD ON MY SHOULDER
I'LL HOLD BACK THE STORM
LIKE A BLANKET WHEN THE NIGHTS GET COLDER
I WILL KEEP YOU WARM

SO YOU CAN DREAM OF THINGS
A ROSE WITHOUT ANY THORNS
LIKE THE GREEN GRASS IN SPRING
Y LOVE IS ALWAYS REBORN

I WON'T LET YOU COME TO HARM
WHEN STILL RIVERS RUN TOO DEEP
I WILL HOLD YOU IN MY ARMS
SLEEP MY DARLING .... GO TO SLEEP

BE AT PEACE WITH THE WORLD
AND PROTECT THE ONES YOU CAN
I'M THINKING OF OUR LITTLE GIRL
THE MIRACLE YOU GAVE YOUR MAN

THAT'S WHY I LOVE YOU
THAT'S WHAT MAKES ME SAY
HONEY YOU ARE SO SPECIAL
IN OH SO MANY WAYS
I WON'T LET YOU COME TO HARM
WHEN WILLOW TREES BEGIN TO WEEP
I WILL HOLD YOU IN MY ARMS
SWEET DREAMS MY DARLING . . . . GO TO SLEEP
SWEET DREAMS MY DARLING . . . . GO TO SLEEP

NOTE# KIND OF MELLOW COUNTRY LULLABY

34

I WANT YOU

AM I ONLY BEING FOOLISH
TO LOVE YOU LIKE I DO
IS IT ONLY WISHFUL THINKING
WISHING THAT YOU LOVED ME TOO

BECAUSE MY HEART STOPS BEATING
WHEN I SEE YOU WALKING BY
YOUR SMILE TAKES MY BREATH AWAY
AND YOUR BEAUTY BLINDS MY EYES

I WANT YOU
I NEED YOU
WHAT MORE CAN I SAY
I LOVE YOU
I HATE YOU
FOR MAKING ME FEEL THIS WAY
I WANT YOU
I NEED YOU
LIKE CLOUDS NEED A SUNNY DAY

AM I JUST BEING LONELY
WISHING I COULD HOLD YOUR HAND
IF YOU WOULD ONLY PHONE ME
I WOULDN'T BE A LONELY MAN

IN DREAMS AND GOLDEN SLUMBER
I'M CUTTING ZEES WITH YOUR SAW
I'M WAITING TO LOAD MY LUMBER
AND STACK IT IN YOUR HALL

I WANT YOU

I NEED YOU

WHAT MORE CAN I SAY

I LOVE YOU

I HATE YOU

FOR MAKING ME FEEL THIS WAY

I WANT YOU

I NEED YOU

LIKE FLOWERS NEED A RAINY DAY

AM I BEING TOO FORWARD

WHEN I SAY THE THINGS I DO

HONEY ARE YOU SO AFRAID

I MIGHT GET THE BEST OF YOU

YOU KNOW THAT I'M EASY

AND YOU'RE PLAYING HARD TO GET

IF YOU WOULD ONLY PLEASE ME

I COULD PROMISE YOU NO REGRETS

I WANT YOU

I NEED YOU

WHAT MORE CAN I SAY

I LOVE YOU

I HATE YOU

FOR MAKING ME FEEL THIS WAY

I WANT YOU

I NEED YOU

LIKE A SONG NEEDS TO PLAY

NOTE# MIDTEMPO COUNTRY/SOFT ROCK MAYBE?/YOU DECIDE
WHAT'S IN YOUR HEAD

35

FALLING FOR YOUR LOVE

LOOK OUT THE WINDOW OF YOUR HEART
TELL YOURSELF WHAT YOU SEE
IS A STRANGER STANDING THERE
OR IS IT ONLY ME

I'M LOOKING OVER THE EDGE
DOWN AT THE FIRE BELOW
I'M JUMPING OFF THE LEDGE
BABY HERE I GO

FALLING
I'M FALLING
I'M FALLING FROM HIGH ABOVE
FALLING
I'M FALLING
I'M FALLING FOR YOUR LOVE
BABY DON'T YOU KNOW
I'M FALLING FOR YOUR LOVE

DON'T SAY IT DOESN'T MATTER
TELL ME THAT YOU CARE
DON'T LET MY HEART SPLATTER
LIKE FIREWORKS IN THE AIR

I NEED YOU SO BAD BABY
I NEED TO BE YOUR MAN
ONLY YOUR LOVE WILL SAVE ME
CATCH ME IF YOU CAN

I'M FALLING
FALLING
I'M FALLING FROM HIGH ABOVE
FALLING
I'M FALLING
I'M FALLING FOR YOUR LOVE
OH YES I KNOW
I'M FALLING FOR YOUR LOVE

REACH OUT YOUR HANDS AND HOLD ME
THAT'S ALL YOU NEED TO DO
SAY THE WORDS YOU HAVEN'T TOLD ME
SAY YOU LOVE ME TOO

GIVE ME YOUR KISSES OH SO FINE
BEFORE I LOSE ALL HOPE
PLEASE TOSS ME A VELVET LOVELINE
BABY THROW ME A ROPE

I'M FALLING
FALLING
I'M FALLING FROM HIGH ABOVE
FALLING
I'M FALLING
I'M FALLING FOR YOUR LOVE
OH HONEY DON'T YOU KNOW
I'M FALLING FOR YOUR LOVE

NOTE# COUNTRY THROUGH AND THROUGH/WHAT ABOUT
YOU?

36

SUPER GRANDMAMA

LITTLE OLD LADY WITH A WALKING STICK
DOES HER TALKING WITH A KUNG FU KICK
IT'S A FACT WHEN THE CRIMINALS ATTACK
HER KARATE CHOPS FEEL LIKE BRICKS

SHE'S MY SUPER GRANDMAMA
SHE CAME FROM BAHAMA
BY WAY OF JAPAN
SHE LEARNED FROM THE MASTER
HOW TO DEAL OUT DISASTER
AND WHIP ANY BAD MAN

I HAVE SEEN THEIR BROKEN BODIES FLYING
WITH BUSTED LIPS AND BLACK EYES CRYING
BEGGING THE COPS TO MAKE HER STOP
WHEN THEY REALIZE THEY MIGHT BE DIEING

NOW EVERY PURSE SNATCHER HIDES IN FEAR
MUGGERS AND THIEVES THEY ALL STEER CLEAR
BECAUSE THEY KNOW WHERE EVER GRANNY GOES
SHE MAKES THE CRIME WAVE DISAPPEAR

SHE'S MY SUPER GRANDMAMA
SHE CAME FROM BAHAMA
BY WAY OF JAPAN
SHE LEARNED FROM THE MASTER
HOW TO DEAL OUT DISASTER
AND WHIP ANY BAD MAN

SHE'S GOT STYLE AND SHE'S GOT GRACE
LIVES ALONE IN THE FAMILY HOMEPLACE
SHE LOVES TO COOK AND READ LAW BOOKS
WHILE RIPPING OFF A BURGLAR'S FACE

SWEET OLD LADY WITH A WALKING STICK
DOES HER TALKING WITH A KUNG FU KICK
IT'S A FACT I NEVER SASS BACK
BECAUSE HER KARATE CHOPS FEEL LIKE BRICKS

SHE'S MY SUPER GRANDMAMA
SHE CAME FROM BAHAMA
BY WAY OF JAPAN
SHE LEARNED FROM THE MASTER
HOW TO DEAL OUT DISASTER
AND WHIP ANY BAD MAN

NOTE# TOBY KEITH COMES TO MIND FIRST BUT ANYONE WITH A
SENSE OF HUMOUR WILL OO/ JIMMY BUFFET MAYBE?

ARE YOU CURIOUS

FOR EYES THAT HAVE TO PEER
SO NOSEY AND SO CURIOUS
SEE THE SMILE THAT DISAPPEARS
ON A FACE SO FURIOUS
BECAUSE NOW YOU HAVE INTRUDED
UPON A LONELY THOUGHT
DISTURBING A VOICE ONCE MUTED
YOUR CURIOSITY HAS BEEN CAUGHT
READING WORDS OF A STRANGER
PICTURES OF PAIN HALF DRAWN
EARS THAT HEAR THE DANGER
STILL THE PEN MARCHES ON
DRAGGING YOU ALONG THE LINES
LIKE MEMORIES FROM YOUR YOUTH
A MYSTERY UNRAVELLING LIKE TWINE
UNTIL THE END REVEALS THE TRUTH
THERE MAY BE DARK SECRETS
HIDING IN A MIND DEPRESSED
THEN AGAIN THERE MAY BE NOTHING
NOTHING MORE AND NOTHING LESS
EXCEPT WHEN LOVE COMES KNOCKING
LIKE GHOSTS ESCAPING FROM A DREAM
YOU MAY FIND THE ANSWER SHOCKING
ONE THAT MAKES YOU SCREAM
IF YOU UNDERSTAND THIS POEM
THEN YOU KNOW WHAT I MEAN

HELL'S FIRE

WALKING DOWN THE ROAD TO ETERNITY
FOOTSTEPS FADING ON THE PATH I TOOK
IF SOMEONE SHOULD GO MISSING ME
THEY WON'T HAVE FAR TO LOOK
I'LL BE THERE IN THE HOT SUMMER AIR
IN EVERY RIVER AND MOUNTAIN STREAM
LIVING IN MEMORIES OF THOSE WHO CARE
RESURRECTED IN A MIDNIGHT DREAM
YOU WON'T KNOW WHERE MY SOUL IS GOING
OR IF I AM REALLY GONE
I MAY BE A SHADOW IN THE DARKNESS
OR THE SUNRISE AT DAWN
YOU KNOW MY BODY WAS CREMATED
AND MY ASHES SCATTERED IN THE WIND
I JUST MIGHT BE REINCARNATED
A BIRD OR MAN'S BEST FRIEND
HELL'S FIRE I MAY BE FEELING
AND FOR ME THERE'S NO REPRIEVE
WHEN THE DEVIL DOES THE DEALING
I MIGHT HAVE ACES UP MY SLEEVE
SO DON'T WORRY ABOUT THE WITCHING HOUR
OR IF YOU SEE MY GHOST
DON'T CRY OR BUY ME FLOWERS
TAKE A DRINK AND MAKE A TOAST
SAY A PRAYER FOR THE LIVING
SING A SONG FOR THE DEAD
I HOPE HEAVEN IS FORGIVING

AND GIVES ME MY DAILY BREAD
SOONER OR LATER IT ALL ENDS
AND WE MUST FACE OUR FEAR
UNTIL THEN LISTEN TO THE WIND
AND THE VOICE WHISPERING IN YOUR EAR

39

COMPLICATIONS

ONCE I THOUGHT I SAW YOU
LIKE A BLUR IN THE NIGHT
JUST ANOTHER MEMORY PASSING THROUGH
LIKE SHADOWS IN THE MOONLIGHT

010 YOU GET WHAT YOU WANTED
TO BE A RICH MAN'S WIFE
IN THE DARK ARE YOU HAUNTED
DOES LOVE COMPLICATE YOUR LIFE

COMPLICATIONS . . . .
A CASTLE ON THE COAST
DO YOU FEEL RIGHT AT HOME
LIVING WITH ALL YOUR GHOSTS

ONCE I THOUGHT I KNEW YOU
BACK IN THE DAYS OF LESS DEMANDS
NCE I THOUGHT I COULD HOLD YOU
BUT YOU SLIPPED RIGHT THROUGH MY HANDS

DID YOU GET WHAT YOU NEEDED
ALL THE PAIN AND DISPAIR
HONEY HAVE YOU NOW SUCCEEDED
IN GETTING YOUR FAIR SHARE

COMPLICATIONS . . . . NOW THAT YOU ARE QUEEN
IN EXCHANGE FOR THE CHANGE
YOU SACRIFICED YOUR DREAMS

ONCE I THOUGHT I SAW YOU

A BLACK CAT IN THE NIGHT

LIKE A COLD WIND BLOWING THROUGH

SEARCHING FOR THE SUNLIGHT

IT COULD BE ME BUT I KNOW IT'S YOU

PRETENDING EVERYTHING'S ALL RIGHT

WAS IT ALL YOU EVER WANTED

TO BE A RICH MAN'S WIFE

IN THE DARK ARE YOU HAUNTED

DO REGRETS CUT LIKE A KNIFE

COMPLICATIONS . . . .

DOES LOVE COMPLICATE YOUR LIFE

CONGRADULATION . . . . TO ALL YOUR LONELY NIGHTS

NOTE# INSPIRED BY THE MOODY BLUES'-NIGHTS IN WHITE SATIN

40

THE BAND

ONE MAN FEINTED WHILE ANOTHER MAN STARED

ONE MAN SMILED AND COMBED HIS HAIR

YOU KNOW WE ALL WERE THERE

THE DAY THE BAND CAME TO TOWN

THEY STOOD UP THERE ON THAT STAGE

PLAYED LIKE DEMONS IN A FIT OF RAGE

THE DANCER GOT NAKED IN HER CAGE

THE DAY THE WALLS CAME TUMBLING DOWN

RIGHT IN THE MIDDLE OF A HEARTBEAT

SOMEBODY KNOCKED ME OFF MY FEET

STOLE MY WOMAN AND TOOK MY SEAT

THERE WAS NOTHING I COULD SAY

I PICKED MYSELF UP OFF THE FLOOR

I BEGGED THE BAND TO PLAY SOME MORE

YOU COULD HEAR ALL THE HIPPIES ROAR

FROM A HUNDRED MILES AWAY

ONE GIRL FEINTED WHILE ANOTHER GIRL STARED

ONE GIRL SCREAMED AND PULLED HER HAIR

YOU KNOW WE ALL WERE THERE

THE DAY THE BAND CAME TO TOWN

THEY STOOD UP THERE ON THAT STAGE

PLAYED EVERY HIT THEY EVER MADE

SOMEONE FREED THE GIRL FROM HER CAGE

THE DAY THE WALLS CAME TUMBLING DOWN

POLICEMAN RUNNING DOWN THE AISLE

HE DIDN'T LIKE MY CROOKED SMILE
PULLED HIS CLUB AND DROVE ME WILD
HIS EYES FILLED WITH HATE
I PICKED MYSELF UP OFF THE FLOOR
HIT HIM WITH MY ICE COLD COORS
YOU SHOULD HAVE HEARD THAT REDNECK ROAR
WHEN I SET THE MATTER STRAIGHT

THE NAKED LADY CUT OUT A LINE
I PASSED THE POT AND POURED THE WINE
I GRABBED HERS AND SHE GRABBED MINE
AS WE DANCED ROUND AND ROUND
BLOWN AWAY BY THAT ROCKING BEAT
FELL OFF OUR CLOUD INTO THE STREET
SNATCHED VICTORY FROM THE JAWS OF DEFEAT
MADE LOVE RIGHT THERE ON THE GROUND
THE DAY THE WALLS CAME TUMBLING DOWN
THE DAY THE BAND CAME TO TOWN

NOTE# INSPIRED IN PART BY DON MCLEAN'S AMERICAN PIE AND
THE BEATLE INVASION

41

LITTLE GREEN MEN

I DIDN'T SPRING FROM THE SEA
A LONG LONG TIME AGO
I DIDN'T SWING WITH THE MONKIES
I CAME FROM A U.F.O.

ALL MY KIN WERE LITTLE GREEN MEN
STANDING ONLY FOUR FEET TALL
THEY BUILT THE PYRIMIDS AND STONEHENGE
AND THE GREAT CHINA WALL
ALL MY KIN WERE LITTLE GREEN MEN
FLYING BEFORE I COULD CRAWL

I HAVE SEEN IN MY DREAMS
EARTH IS JUST ANOTHER STAR
MAD SCIENCETIST CAME WITH THEIR LASER BEAMS
GAVE BIRTH TO WHO WE ARE

I FELT THEIR TINY HANDS
DIGGING DEEP INSIDE MY BRAIN
THEY PLANTED SEEDS ACROSS THE LAND
AND BROUGHT DOWN THE RAIN

ALL MY KIN WERE LITTLE GREEN MEN
FROM THE CRADLE TO THE GRAVE
THEY BUILT THE PYRIMIDS AND STONEHENGE
WITHOUT THE HELP OF SLAVES
WE WERE ONLY EXPERIMENTS BACK THEN
TEST TUBE BABIES BORN IN CAVES

EVERY YEAR THEY VISIT HERE
JUST TO SEE WHAT'S WRONG
THEY DISAPPEAR INTO THE ATMOSPHERE
WHEN THE HEAR THIS SONG

WE DIDN'T SPRING FROM THE SEA
A LONG LONG TIME AGO
WE DIDN'T SWING WITH THE MONKIES
WE CAME FROM U.F.O.S

ALL MY KIN WERE LITTLE GREEN MEN
STANDING ONLY FOUR FEET TALL
THEY BUILT THE PYRIMIDS AND STONEHENGE
AND THE GREAT CHINA WALL
ALL MY KIN WERE LITTLE GREEN MEN
FLYING BEFORE I COULD CRAWL

NOTE# KIND OF SILLY CONTEMPORARY COUNTRY SONG

42

OH THAT SMELL

AFTER WORK I DRIVE MY CAR AND PARK IT
IN THE ALLEY BY THE BAY
THE SIGN SAYS WELCOME TO FREDDIE'S FISH MARKET
I HOPE YOU HAVE A ROTTEN DAY

THAT'S HER LOUSY WAY OF JOKING
SHE LIKES TO MAKE ME MAD
WITH HER WHISKEY BREATH AND SMOKING
MY HEALTH IS TURNING BAD

OH THAT SMELL I KNOW SO WELL
LOVE IS STINKING UP MY LIFE
MY LIPS PUCKER AND MY EYES SWELL
WHEN I KISS MY CRAZY WIFE
WHEN SHE BURNS DINNER ALL TO HELL
I DUCK FROM THE FLYING KNIFE

WHY DON'T SHE DO THE LAUNDRY
WHY DOES SHE TREAT ME MEAN
I CALL HER A FREAK OF NATURE
SHE CALLS ME MISTER CLEAN

WHY DON'T SHE DO THE DISHES
THEY ARE BREAKING DOWN THE SINK
WHY DON'T SHE GRANT MY WISHES
\BEFORE SHE TAKES ANOTHER DRINK

OH THAT SMELL I KNOW SO WELL
BUT I STILL LOVE MY WIFE

I'M LIKE A MAN STUCK IN JAIL
I'VE BEEN SENTENCED HERE FOR LIFE
WHEN MY BABY RINGS THE DINNER BELL
I STAB MY PRIDE WITH A KNIFE

WHY CAN'T I CATCH HER IN THE TUB
SO I CAN SCRUB HER HIDE
WHY SHOULD SHE BE MAD ON HER BIRTHDAY
I BOUGHT HER A BOX OF TIDE
NOW WHEN I EAT HER COOKING
I HAVE TO HOLD MY BREATH
SHE SAYS HONEY AINT IT GOOD LOOKING
I SAY IT SCARES ME TO DEATH

OH THAT SMELL I KNOW SO WELL
IT'S CALLED THE PERFUME OF LIFE
MY BED BOUNCES AND BREAKS THE RAILS
WHEN I KISS MY CRAZY WIFE
WHEN SHE COOKS UP HER MAGIC SPELL
I WHIP OUT MY POCKET KNIFE

NOTE# REWRITTEN TONED DOWN VERSION FROM THE ORIGINAL
IN MY BOOK THE EMPTY ROOM@AUTHORHOUSE.COM/UPBEAT

43

SONGS IN THE DARK

CHILDREN FILLING UP THEIR SACKS
DRESSED IN SCARY COSTUMES
BLACK CATS AND VAMPIRE BATS
WITCHES ON THEIR BROOMS
MY SPRIT FLYS WITH CRYING EYES
FAR FROM THIS LONELY TOMB

YOU STILL LOOK GOOD LIKE I KNEW YOU WOULD
HE SAME AS YOU DID BACK THEN
A REFLECTION IN THE GLASS FROM DAYS GONE PASSED
I'M ON THE OUTSIDE LOOKING IN

INVISIBLE HANDS STRIKE UP THE BAND
BALLADS FROM A BROKEN HEART
MIDNIGHT SERENADES ABOUT THE LOVE WE MADE
SONGS IN THE DARK
SONGS IN THE DARK

MY SKELETON REMAINS WRAPPED IN RUSTY CHAINS
FROM ALL THE TEARS I CRIED BEFORE
I SEE WEREWOLVES WALKING DOWN MEMORY LANE
GHOSTS AND GOBLINS AT YOUR DOOR
GIVE THEM CANDY SO THEY DON'T COMPLAIN
THE GRIM REAPER BEGS FOR MORE

THERE'S A VOICE CALLING OUT TO YOU
IF YOU TAKE THE TIME TO LISTEN
WORDS ON THE WIND TELLING YOU AGAIN

IT'S A CRIME WE AINT KISSING

INVISIBLE HANDS STRIKE UP THE BAND
BALLADS FROM A BROKEN HEART
MIDNIGHT SERENADES ABOUT THE LOVE WE MADE
SONGS IN THE DARK
SONGS IN THE DARK
TINY LITTLE DEMONS HUNGRY AND SCREAMING
THEY MAKE YOUR DOORBELL RING
YOU CAN DROP A BOMB ON A PEEPING TOM
BABY I WOULDN'T FEEL A THING

I'M PARALIZED WITH FEAR TO BE SO NEAR
SO CLOSE AND YET SO FAR AWAY
I WILL HAUNT YOUR HOUSE FOR YEARS
AND LOVE YOU MORE EACH DAY

INVISIBLE HANDS STRIKE UP THE BAND
BALLADS FROM A BROKEN HEART
MIDNIGHT SERENADES ABOUT THE LOVE WE MADE
SONGS IN THE DARK
SONGS IN THE DARK

NOTE# GOT THE IDEA FROM THE GARY ALLAN SONG-SMOKE
RINGS IN THE DARK AND HOLLOWEEN/REWRITE FROM THE
ORIGINAL IN (THE EMPTY ROOM)@AUTHORHOUSE.COM/

44

9/11 ALWAYS REMEMBER

THE WAR BIRDS OF TERROR FLEW
LIKE ARROWS IN THE WIND
STRAIGHT INTO THE RED WHITE AND BLUE
A NATION BECAME UNHINGED
HOPEFULLY ALL THE HOSTAGES KNEW
HEAVEN WOULD LET THEM IN

THROUGH THE SMOKE AND FIRE
THE OLD AND THE YOUNG
WE RAISED OUR FLAG EVEN HIGHER
IN DEFIANCE FOR THE FALLEN ONES
FROM THE RUBBLE AND THE RUIN
SO MANY HEROES SPRUNG

THE WAR BIRDS OF TERROR CRASHED
AGAINST OUR WALLS OF STEEL
HEARTS WERE BROKE AND DREAMS WERE SMASHED
BUT THEY DIDN'T BREAK OUR WILL
THE RICH THE POOR AND THE MIDDLECLASS
NOW KNOW THE THREAT IS REAL

LOVED ONES LOST BUT NOT FORGOTTEN
BY THE MILLIONS THAT REMAIN
A SINGLE VOICE ROSE UP FROM THE LAND
NO ONE SHOULD DIE IN VAIN
A MIGHTY FIST THAT NOW DEMANDS
RETRIBUTION FOR ALL THE PAIN

THEY UNDERESTIMATED OUR RESOLVE
AND OUR STRENGTH TO REBUILD
A BETTER PLACE FOR US TO LIVE
BECAUSE FREEDOM CAN'T BE KILLED
NAMES THAT ARE ENSHRINED FOREVER
A MONUMENT ON THE BATTLEFIELD

FORCED TO TURN LOOSE OUR COURAGE
WHILE OUR WOUNDED NATION MENDS
TODAY WE CELEBRATE THE NEWS
OUR ENEMY HAS MET HIS END
NOW WITH PRIDE WE STEP ASIDE
ALWAYS TO REMEMBER WHEN

45

YEARS AGO

MY BEAUTIFUL MOTHER WAS A WITCH
CASTING SPELLS NIGHT AND DAY
SHE WOULD RATHER FIGHT THAN SWITCH
OR CHANGE HER EVIL WAYS
I THOUGHT LIFE WAS A BITCH
BUT WHO WAS I TO SAY

I WAS VERY YOUNG
WHAT DID I KNOW
WITH HER SHARP TONGUE
SHE CUT ME HEAD TO TOE
IF NOT FOR THE FOOD SHE BRUNG
I WOULD HAVE DIED YEARS AGO

I THOUGHT MY DAD TO BE UNKIND
WHEN HE MADE ME PLAY
LITTLE LEAGUE AND GAMES IN MY MIND
AND HOW A BOY SHOULD PRAY
HE LOVED TO PREACH WHILE DRINKING WINE
I HEARD HIS SERMONS EVERYDAY

I WAS VERY YOUNG
WHAT DID I KNOW
UNTIL MY BELLS WERE RUNG
SCHOOL WAS JUST FOR SHOW
WHEN THE SPOONS AND FORKS WERE FLUNG
I LEARNED TO DUCK YEARS AGO

I THOUGHT THAT NO ONE LOVED ME
I CRIED NIGHT AND DAY
I CURSED THE SKY ABOVE ME
WITH WORDS I SHOULDN'T SAY
I THOUGHT THAT NO ONE LOVED ME
AND I WAS IN THE WAY

I WAS VERY YOUNG
WHAT DID I KNOW
LIFE HAD JUST BEGUN
THERE WAS ROOM TO GROW
WHEN I COMPLAINED AT TWENTYONE
THEY SMILED AND LET ME GO

46

THE FUNNY FARM

THEY LET US WATCH CARTOONS
AND PAINT PICTURES ON THE WALL
WE TAKE A NAP AT NOON
WITH OUR TOYS AND RUBBER BALLS

THEN IT'S OFF TO WORK
THEN IT'S OFF TO PLAY
SMILELY FACES ON OUR SHIRTS
CRACKING UP ALONG THE WAY

CURIOUS EYES LOOKING FOR THE PRIZE
IN A BOX OF LUCKY CHARMS
MICKEY MOUSE IS IN THE HOUSE
DOWN ON THE FUNNY FARM

YOU KNOW WE HAVE OUR HEROES
SCOOBY 000 AND FRIENDS
SPACEMAN COUNTS DOWN TO ZERO
ARMS FLAPPING IN THE WIND

LIVING INSIDE OUR HAPPY WORLD
TUCKED SAFELY OUT OF VIEW
NOT JUST FOR BOYS AND GIRLS
GROWNUPS LIVE HERE TOO

TOM AND JERRY AND THE TOOTH FAIRY
ALL HAVE TATOOS ON THEIR ARM
OLD MAN MOSES PLANTS PLASTIC ROSES
DOWN ON THE FUNNY FARM

DAFFY DUCK DRIVES A BEAT UP TRUCK
THROUGH A BED OF DAFFODILS
ELMER FUDD MARCHES THROUGH THE MUD
LOOKING FOR HIS HUNTING SKILLS

BUGS BUNNY WITH CARROTS AND MONEY
HE SHARES WITH MISTER ED
WHICH OF COURSE IS A TALKING HORSE
IN A BARN PAINTED RED
MOTHER GOOSE SHE JUST BROKE LOOSE
NO ONE SOUNDS THE ALARM
WE ALL KNOW WHERE SHE GOES
DOWN ON THE FUNNY FARM

YOU ARE THERE AND I AM HERE
TOGETHER IN THIS NURSERY RHYME
FOOL ON THE HILL AND STRAWBERRY FIELDS
THE BEATLES SING AT DINNER TIME

THAT'S WHEN WE LAUGH AT EVERY TUNE
AND THROW FOOD AGAINST THE WALL
BETTY BOOP AND THE BIG BABBOON
GOT MARRIED IN THE DINING HALL

IF YOU LOOK YOU CAN ALWAYS FIND
A PLACE SAFE FROM HARM
WE ALL ARE CHILDREN IN OUR MIND
COMMITTED TO THE FUNNY FARM

NOTE# HOPE YOU HAVE A GOOD LAUGH AND SOMEONE HAS
THE NERVE TO SING THIS SILLY SONG.

47

BRAIN DEAD

WHO'S THE FACE BEHIND THE MASK
WHO'S THE FACE BEHIND THE MASK
WILL THE ANSWERS COME WHEN YOUR BRAIN IS NUMB
FROM ALL THE QUESTIONS PEOPLE ASK

HEAR THE VOICES IN THE WALLS
FEAR THE VOICES IN THE HALL
YOU FIGHT YOUR WAR BEHIND CLOSED DOORS
EVERY NIGHT YOU LOSE A LITTLE MORE

AND WHEN YOUR HEART BREAKS INSIDE YOUR LONELY ROOM
AND THERE'S NO TIME LEFT TO KILL
AND WHEN YOUR BED BECOMES THE DUNGEON OF DOOM
I'LL SAY A PRAYER FOR ALL THE LOONEY TOONS

WITH YOUR BILLS NEATLY STACKED
YOU MOUNT YOUR LAST ATTACK
IN TATTERED RAGS YOU RAISE YOUR FLAG
BROWN BOTTLE COURAGE IN A PAPER BAG

YOU BATTLE FOR CONTROL
BUT THERE'S NO VICTORY
THERE'S A STRANGER IN YOUR BED
SLEEPING WITH THE ENEMY

AND WHEN YOU SURRENDER INSIDE A PADDED ROOM
AND YOU WITHDRAW FROM THE PILLS
AND WHEN YOUR DREAMS DIE A DAY TOO SOON
I'LL SAY A PRAYER FOR ALL THE LOONEY TOONS

(END)
AND WHEN YOUR MUSIC BOX GOES BOOM
NO MORE SONGS FOR ALL YOU LOONEY TOONS

NOTE# MY VERSION OF THE PINK FLOYD CLASSIC-BRAIN DAMAGE(DARK SIDE OF THE MOON) ONE OF MY FAVORITE ALBUMS

48

LADY KILLER

HERE'S A WARNING TO ALL THE WOMEN
WITH DIAMONDS BIG AS STARS
MANY HAVE TRIED TO KEEP ME BRIBED
WITH MONEY AND LUXURY CARS

FALLING IN LOVE IS ALWAYS EASY
WHEN YOUR LONELY AND BORED
MANY HAVE TRIED TO KEEP ME HOGTIED
BEHIND THEIR BEDROOM DOOR

MICHAEL JACKSON WAS THE THRILLER
BUT I'M THE LADY KILLER
BREAKING HEARTS AND MORE
ES I'M THE LADY KILLER
THE LOVE YOU'RE DIEING FOR

I'M WANTED DEAD OR ALIVE
BY THE GODS OF JEALOUSY
SINGLE WOMEN AND HORNY WIVES
GET THE BEST OF ME

TAKE YOUR HANDS AND COP A FEEL
ALL MY LOVE IS FREE
HONEY I'M THE REAL DEAL
SEXY AS I CAN BE

MICHAEL JACKSON WAS THE THRILLER
BUT I'M THE LADY KILLER
LEAVING HEARTS IN MISERY

YES I'M THE LADY KILLER
THE DROWNING POOL OF ECSTACY

SNIPERS SHOOTING FROM THE ROOFTOPS
WOMEN BEGGING ME TO STAY
HEY CHASE ME TO THE BUS STOP
CRY WHEN I GET AWAY
COUNTRY QUEENS AND WIVES OF KINGS
SAVE THE JEWELS IN YOUR CROWN
I DON'T NEED A SINGLE THING
TO CHAIN MY SPIRIT DOWN

MICHAEL JACKSON WAS THE THRILLER
BUT I'M THE LADY KILLER
BREAKING HEARTS IN EVERY TOWN
YES I'M THE LADY KILLER
THE LOVE YOU THOUGHT YOU FOUND

NOTE# UPBEAT CONTEMPORARY COUNTRY/SOFT ROCK-POP
MAYBE

49

WELCOME TO MY DAYDREAM

I HEAR THE GHOST OF STEVEN
SINGING A SONG THAT ROCKS
I HEAR ALICE COOPER GETTING EVEN
ON THAT OLD JUKE BOX

I WON'T CONCEDE ONLY WOMEN BLEED
WHEN NO LOVE REMAINS
I AM A MAN WHO UNDERSTANDS
HOW TO FEEL THE PAIN

WELCOME TO MY DAYDREAM
FULL OF JAGGED SCARS
NO ONE CAN SAVE ME
FROM THIS WHISKEY BAR
WELCOME TO MY DAYDREAM
WHITE LIGHTNING IN A JAR

DEVIL'S FOOD IS ON THE TABLE
BLACK WIDOW FEEDS ON DEATH
BECAUSE SOME FOLKS ARE NEVER ABLE
TO CATCH A SOBER BREATH

I FIGHT MY WAR WITH WORDS
WHILE MUSIC RAPES THE AIR
I KNOW IT SOUNDS ABSURD
WRITING SONGS ABOUT DISPAIR

WELCOME TO MY DAYDREAM
WHERE LIFE IS SO BIZARRE

CAN YOU SEE ME
FROM WHERE YOU ARE
WELCOME TO MY DAYDREAM
DEAD DRUNK IN MY CAR

THE AWAKENING OF SAVAGE JEALOUSY
SPILLED BLOOD UPON THE ROSE
I THOUGHT COLD ETHYL LOVED ME
UNTIL SHE BROKE MY NOSE
DEPARTMENT OF YOUTH COULDN'T CHANGE ME
INTO SOMETHING THAT I'M NOT
WHEN I STARTED ACTING STRANGELY
SHE LEFT ME HERE TO ROT

WELCOME TO MY DAYDREAM
HIGH AMONG THE STARS
COME AND JOIN ME
THE MAD MAN FROM MARS
WELCOME TO MY DAYDREAM
WHERE FOOLS FLY TOO FAR

NOTE# INSPIRED BY ALICE COOPER SONGS ON HIS WELCOME TO
MY NIGHTMARE ALBUM

50

THE ATTIC

THE ATTIC THE ATTIC
A GHOST IS IN THE ATTIC
KICKING ALL MY JUNK AROUND
THE ATTIC THE ATTIC
A GHOST IS IN THE ATTIC
MAKING STRANGE AND CREEPY SOUNDS

A HAUNTING A HAUNTING
I WONDER WHAT IT'S WANTING
FOR WHOM DOES IT GRIEVE
A HAUNTING A HAUNTING
I KNOW WHAT IT'S WANTING
IT WANTS ME TO LEAVE

I HAVE HEARD A BABY CRYING
I HAVE SEEN A SHADOW FLYING
STRAIGHT UP MY CREAKY STAIRS
I HAVE FELT MY BED SHAKE
I HAVE SEEN MY DISHES BREAK
FACES FLOATING IN THE AIR
ONCE I FELT A COLD KISS
RIGHT BEFORE THE DAGGER MISSED
SOMETHING TELLS ME TO BEWARE

THE SPIRIT THE SPIRIT
EVERY DAY I'M NEAR IT
FOOTSTEPS WALKING DOWN THE HALL
THE SPIRIT THE SPIRIT

EVERY NIGHT I HEAR IT
THE VOICE INSIDE THE WALL

THE ATTIC THE ATTIC
THE GHOSTS ARE IN THE ATTIC
MAKING STRANGE AND CREEPY SOUNDS
THE ATTIC THE ATTIC
THE GHOSTS FLY FROM THE ATTIC
CHASING ME OUT OF TOWN

51

TIME

THERE'S NO USE IN COMPLAINING
WHAT GOOD WOULD IT DO
OUTSIDE THE SKY IS RAINING
THE SUN HAS SET ON YOU

ACROSS THE MOUNTAINS THE SHADOWS FLY
LIKE GHOSTS IN THE WIND
YOU THINK OF DAYS GONE BY
AS THE DARKNESS CLOSES IN

TIME . . . .
YOU THOUGHT THAT YOU HAD PLENTY
TIME . . . .
NOW YOU KNOW YOU DON'T HAVE ANY
TIME . . . .
COACH POTATOE SITTING ON YOUR PENNIES
SPENDING ALL YOUR TIME

TIRED EYES GLUED TO THE TUBE
T.V. DINNERS AND CHEAP WINE
YOU'RE JUST LIKE EBENEEZER SCROOGE
WORKING HARD TO SAVE A DIME

SOME SAY WHEN YOU'RE OLD AND GREY
THE TRUTH WILL HUNT YOU DOWN
AND YOU WILL PAY FOR THE YESTERDAYS
AND THE TOMORROWS YOU NEVER FOUND

TIME . . . .

YOU THOUGHT THAT YOU HAD PLENTY

TIME . . . .

NOW YOU KNOW YOU DON'T HAVE ANY

TIME . . . .

COACH POTATOE SITTING ON YOUR PENNIES

SPENDING ALL YOUR TIME THERE'S NO USE IN COMPLAINING

WHEN DREAMS DON'T COME TRUE

IF YOU LISTEN I'M EXPLAINING

EXACTLY WHAT YOU SHOULD DO

CLIMB THE MOUNTAIN INTO THE SKY

AND FIND THE SUN AGAIN

BUT IF YOU'RE AFRAID TO TRY

HERE'S HOW YOUR LIFE WILL END

TIME . . . .

YOU THOUGHT THAT YOU HAD PLENTY

TIME . . . .

LAZY LOSERS FIND THEY DON'T HAVE ANY

TIME . . . .

ROTTEN POTATOES AINT WORTH A PENNY

WASTING AWAY IN TIME

NOTE# KIND OF SOFT ROCK BALLAD/MOODY BLUES(NIGHTS IN
WHITE SATIN)STYLE OR PINK FLOYD(DARK SIDE OF THE MOON)
STYLE

52

ADULTERY

I CAN'T BELIEVE YOU WOULD EVER LEAVE
TEARS CLOUD MY POINT OF VIEW
I'M NOT SURE THERE IS A CURE
FOR THE DOUBTS I HAVE IN YOU

ALL MY HOPES ARE IN YOUR HANDS
RIDING ON THE WINGS OF DESTINY
THROUGH THE HOLE IN MY WEDDING BAND
THE RUMOURS BUZZ LIKE BEES

I WANT TO KNOW WHERE YOU GO
WHEN YOU'RE NOT WITH ME
DON'T YOU KNOW I LOVE YOU SO
WHERE EVER YOU MAY BE
LET'S GO BACK TO DAYS OF OLD
BEFORE YOU LEARNED ADULTERY

I'M HANGING ON TO WHAT IS GONE
LIKE OLD TIME ROCK AND ROLL
SMILE AND WAVE YOUR MAGIC WAND
PLEASE SAVE MY TORTURED SOUL

THE GOSSIP MOUNGERS HOUND MY DOOR
LIKE A BUNCH OF THIEVES
MY MIND IS TRAPPED FOREVER MORE
IN THE WEB YOUR SPIDER WEAVES

I WANT TO KNOW WHERE YOU GO
WHEN YOU'RE NOT WITH ME

DON'T YOU KNOW I LOVE YOU SO
WHERE EVER YOU MAY BE
LET'S GO BACK TO DAYS OF OLD
BEFORE YOU LEARNED ADULTERY

PROVE TO ME YOU WILL NEVER LEAVE
YOU CAN CHANGE MY POINT OF VIEW
I'M NOT SURE THERE IS A CURE
WHEN THE HEART BREAKS IN TWO
ALL THE PIECES ARE IN YOUR HANDS
PUT ME BACK TOGETHER PLEASE
I AM JUST HALF A MAN
DOWN HERE ON MY KNEES

I WANT TO KNOW WHERE YOU GO
WHEN YOU'RE NOT WITH ME
DON'T YOU KNOW I LOVE YOU SO
WHERE EVER YOU MAY BE
LET'S GO BACK TO DAYS OF OLD
BEFORE YOU LEARNED ADULTERY

NOTE# INSPIRED BY URIAH HEEP'S (PARADISE THE SPEIL) FROM
THEIR DEMONS AND WIZARDS ALBUM/ROCK SONG

53

WAR

I'M SURE YOU HAVE HEARD BEFORE
LET'S MAKE LOVE INSTEAD OF WAR

WE LET POLITICIANS PICK OUR POCKETS
TO PAY THEIR RAISE WE CAN'T AFFORD
SO THEY CAN BUY THEIR ROCKETS
BLOW THE POOR RIGHT OUT THE DOOR
THEY TAKE THEIR CONSCIENCE AND LOCK IT
FAR BELOW THE WHITE HOUSE FLOOR

I'M SURE YOU HAVE HEARD BEFORE
THERE'S NO LOVE WHEN MAKING WAR

I KNOW IT'S HARD TO UNDERSTAND
THE LAWS THAT RULE THE LAND
AND WHY THERE'S NO HOPE ALIVE
I VOTED TO SAVE THE COMMON MAN
IN HIS CONSTANT STRUGGLE TO SURVIVE
BUT CONGRESS ALWAYS HAS A PLAN
TO HELP BIG BUSINESS THRIVE

I'M SURE YOU HAVE HEARD BEFORE
POVERTY IS THE CHILD OF WAR

WHY DON'T THEY SPEND OUR MONEY
REBUILD THE LAND OF MILK AND HONEY
THE WAY THINGS USE TO BE
THERE ARE NATIONS THAT THINK IT'S FUNNY
WHEN OUR LEADERS JUMP AROUND LIKE BUNNIES

AND SEND OUR SOLDIERS OVERSEAS

I'M SURE YOU HAVE HEARD BEFORE
BROKEN PROMISES OF NO MORE WAR

NOW I WILL END THIS TALE
WITHOUT MY SOUL TO SELL
I GAVE IT TO THE PRESIDENT
HE TOLD ME NOT TO YELL
AND THINGS WERE GOING REALLY WELL
WHERE ALL THE BOMBS WERE SENT
I'M HANGING ON TOOTH AND NAIL
WITH THE HOMELESS HERE IN JAIL
BECAUSE WE COULDN'T PAY OUR RENT

I'M SURE YOU HAVE HEARD BEFORE
WE ARE THE SPOILS OF WAR

NOTE# STILL STUCK IN THE SIXTIES KIND OF PROTEST SONG/
MUST BE THE HIPPIE IN ME

54

ONE GREAT SONG

FOR THOSE THAT MISS THE BOAT
THEY HAVE MADE THEIR CHOICE
HERE'S THE LYRICS THAT I WROTE
STILL SEARCHING FOR A VOICE

EVEN THOUGH MY WORDS ARE NEVER BOUGHT
MY LIPS REFUSE TO CUSS
I STILL RIDE MY TRAIN OF THOUGHTS
WHILE OTHERS MISS THE BUS
THEY NEVER REALIZE WHAT LIES INSIDE
ONE GREAT SONG IN ALL OF US

WE CAN SING OF LOVE AND PEACE
AND THE FUTURE OF HUMANITY
OR WE CAN WAIT FOR OUR RELEASE
FROM THE PRISON OF PROCRASTINY

I KNOW I'VE SAID IT ALL BEFORE
AT LEAST A THOUSAND TIMES
HERE'S THE HIT YOUR LOOKING FOR
BURIED DEEP INSIDE THE RYHMES

LIKE THE LOTTERY TICKETS THAT YOU BUY
DISAPPOINTMENT IS ALL YOU WIN
YOUR LUCKY NUMBER IS NINE TO FIVE
AS YOU WORK TOWARDS THE END
YOU CAN DO IT IF YOU TRY
ONE GREAT SONG FOR ALL YOUR FRIENDS

I'M GIVING YOU ALL THE WORDS
AND ALL MY IMAGINATION TOO
I HOPE YOUR EARS HAVE
HEARD THE MUSIC INSIDE OF YOU

GRAB THE MICROPHONE WITH BOTH HANDS
AND SING A COUNTRY TUNE
THEN ALL YOUR FANS WILL UNDERSTAND
THE MAN IN THE MOON

EVEN IF THESE LINES ARE NEVER BOUGHT
MY LI PS REFUSE TO CUSS
I STILL RIDE MY TRAIN OF THOUGHTS
WHILE OTHERS MISS THE BUS
THEY NEVER REALIZE WHAT LIES INSIDE
ONE GREAT SONG IN ALL OF US

NOTE# WISHFUL THINKING /HOW ABOUT YOU?/NO I'M NOT
DRINKING/ BUT I COULD USE A BREW

55

WITH PEN IN HAND

IT'S HARD TO EXPLAIN THE MELODIES IN MY BRAIN
SO YOU CAN SING ALONG
WITH PEN IN HAND COMES THE MUSIC MAN
WRITING YOU ANOTHER SONG

I HOPE THAT I DON'T CONFUSE YOU
WITH LESSONS I'VE BEEN TAUGHT
I HOPE THAT I DON'T LOSE YOU
AMONG ALL MY CRAZY THOUGHTS

IT'S ONLY ME THAT YOU SEE
TRAPPED BETWEEN THE LINES
IN CHAINS I CAN'T BREAK FREE
FROM THIS CURSE OF MINE

I HOPE I MAKE YOU LAUGH
I HOPE I MAKE YOU CRY
FOLLOW ME DOWN THE GARDEN PATH
WHERE TRUTH IS MIXED WITH LIES

MUGSHOTS IN THE PHOTOGRAPHS
HIDING BEHIND THEIR ALIBIES
LIVING HERE IN THE AFTERMATH
WHERE IMAGINATION NEVER DIES
IF YOUR CURIOUSITY SHOULD EVER ASK
THIS WOULD BE MY REPLY

I HOPE THAT I AMUSE YOU
AND IT COMES AS NO SURPRISE

WHEN BATMAN SWINGS INTO VIEW
THE JOKER FACES HIS DEMISE

WONDERWOMAN IN HER SEE THROUGH JET
CHASING DOWN ALL THE THUGS
SHE SURE LOOKS GOOD SOAKING WET
OH WHAT A PAIR OF JUGS

IT'S HARD TO EXPLAIN THE PLEASURE AND THE PAIN
WHAT IS AND ISN'T REAL
ONE MORE TUNE FROM A FLOCK OF LOONS
LANDING ON MY WINDOW SILL

THE VOICES CALL AS THE DARKNESS FALLS
HAUNTING ME ALL NIGHT LONG
WITH PEN IN HAND COMES THE MUSIC
MAN TURNING POETRY INTO SONG

56

TURNING DESERTS INTO MUD

LOW LIFE LOOKING FOR LOOT
INNOCENT VICTIMS PREYED UPON
WITH BLOOD ON THEIR BOOTS
THE ARMY MARCHES ON

IN THE NAME OF FREEDOM
SO THE POLITICIANS SAY
BUT DO WE REALLY NEED THEM
SHOWING US THE WAY

TEARS TURN DESERTS INTO MUD
DESOLATION AND DESEASE
THE MOON TURNS INTO BLOOD
DRIPPING DOWN ON DEMOCRACY
SO KINGS CAN KEEP THEIR KINGDOMS
WE DEFEND THEIR LIBERTY

IT'S NEVER NICE TO SACRIFICE
ANOTHER MOTHER'S SON
OR DAUGHTERS WHO PAY THE PRICE
FOR MEDALS THAT THEY WON

TRYING TO CHANGE RELIGIOUS MINDS
WAGING A WAR WE CANNOT WIN
IT'S LIKE LEADING THE BLIND
STRAIGHT INTO THE LION'S DEN

TEARS TURN DESERTS INTO MUD
NATIONS FLAUNT THEIR INDIGNITY

OUR FUTURE IS WRITTEN IN BLOOD
FOR ALL THE WORLD TO SEE
SO KINGS CAN BUILD THEIR KINGDOMS
ON TOP OF MISERY

I WONDER WHY IT'S SO HARD
STAYING OUT OF FOREIGN AFFAIRS
WE SHOULD CLEAN UP OUR OWN YARD
BEFORE WE CLEAN UP THEIR'S

TEARS TURN DESERTS INTO MUD
AFTER THE KILLING SPREE
BUSY BODIES IN OUR BLOOD
STICKING OUR NOSE WHERE IT SHOULDN'T BE
SO KINGS CAN CLAIM THEIR KINGDOMS
AND LAUGH WHEN WE LEAVE

TEARS TURN DESERTS INTO MUD
NOW WE ALL ARE FREE
THE MOON TURNS INTO BLOOD
ANOTHER BIBLE PROPHECY
WASHED AWAY BY THE FLOOD
EVERY TRACE OF HUMANITY

NOTE# POETIC NONSENSE OR THE TRUTH?

57

FAMILY AND FRIENDS

THIS BOOK THAT I'M WRITING
FOR FAMILY AND FRIENDS
I DEDICATE TO COWBOY TOM
AND MY SISTER LISA LYNN

BECAUSE THEY HAVE HELPED ME
IN MY TIME OF NEED
IF NOT FOR THEIR LOVE
WHERE WOULD I BE

I LOST MY BEST FRIEND RANDY
TO THE DEVIL'S ALCOHOL
I CAN STILL HEAR HIM LAUGHING
AND SEE HIM PLAYING BALL

I'M STILL PERPLEXED BY MY BROTHER REX
BUT IT'S REALLY NO BIG DEAL
WHEN MY LIFE WAS A NERVOUS WRECK
HE TOOK ME IN UNTIL I HEALED

MY SISTER SANDY CAME IN HANDY
WHEN I COULD BARELY CRAWL
SHE CAME AND CLEANED UP MY HOUSE
AND SHE PAINTED ALL MY WALLS

I WANT THEM ALL TO KNOW
IN MY TIME OF NEED
IF NOT FOR THEIR LOVE
WHERE WOULD I BE

THAT CRAZY GIRL I CALL CHERYL
WE SELDOM HAVE MUCH TO SAY
BUT I KNOW IF I SHOULD ASK HER
SHE WOULD COME HERE RIGHT AWAY

SUZI Q IS YOU KNOW WHO
THE KEEPER OF MY HEART
THEN THERE'S SEAN AND CHARLES ANDREW
CHILDREN ARE THE BEST PART

THEN THERE'S MANDY AND BRANDI
AND DENNIS THE MENACE TOO
IF NOT FOR FAMILY AND FRIENDS
WHAT WOULD A PERSON DO

THERE'S TOO MANY NAMES TO MENTION
I HAVE ONLY MENTIONED A FEW
BEFORE I LOSE YOUR ATTENTION
I'D LIKE TO THANK ALL OF YOU

58

ON THE WINDS OF CHANGE

YOU HIDE YOUR EYES BEHIND STAINED GLASS
TO NEVER KNOW WHAT LIES OUTSIDE
YOU LEAVE YOUR PRAYERS AT THE ALTER
AND LET YOUR GOD DECIDE

I TRIED TO MAKE YOU LOVE ME
BEFORE YOU STARTED ACTING STRANGE
AND PLACED A HIGHER POWER ABOVE ME
ON THE WINDS OF CHANGE

I TRIED TO MAKE YOU HOLD ME
AND KEEP EVERYTHING THE SAME
I ALMOST DIED WHEN YOU TOLD ME
RELIGION MAKES YOUR HEART REFRAIN

THERE'S NOTHING WRONG WITH THE CHURCH
IF THAT'S YOUR CUP OF TEA
BUT WHY LEAVE LOVE IN THE LURCH
WHEN YOU WALK AWAY FROM ME

I TRIED TO MAKE YOU SAVE ME
FROM THE BOUNDRIES THAT REMAIN
AND THE MEMORIES THAT NOW ENSLAVE ME
ON THE WINDS OF CHANGE

COME YEA ALL THE FAITHFUL
MINSTRELS AND MINISTERS ORDAINED
BROKEN HEARTS ARE NEVER GRATEFUL
WHEN THEY FLY AWAY IN PAIN

I TRIED TO MAKE YOU SEE ME
BEFORE THE CHURCHBELLS RANG
AND YOU THREW YOURSELF FREELY
ON THE WINDS OF CHANGE

THERE'S NOTHING BETTER THAN A LOVE SONG
WHEN THE WORDS ARE ALL ARRANGED
UNLESS SOMETHING BETTER COMES ALONG
ON THE WINDS OF CHANGE

THE TRAVELING HILLBILLY
14-CO TRACKS

59   HE HILLBILLY SONG-1

60   LOVE COMES IN MANY COLORS-2

61   SHE'S GONE FISHING-3

62   EARS IN THE WIND-4

63   MAMA'S EYES-5

64   MACHO WOMAN-6

65   DEVIL IN THE DARK-7

66   AT'S IN THE FIRE-8

67   POUND ME LIKE A NAIL-9

68   MY PIE-10

69   0H HALLOWEENIE-11

70   SEASONS OUT OF TIME-12

71   I'M GOING HOME-13

72   LOGAN TOWN—14

THE HILLBILLY SONG

WAY UP HIGH ON THAT MOUNTAIN
THERE STANDS A SHACK AMONG THE PINES
WHERE WE WASHED OUR DIRTY FACES
WITH WATER WE PACKED FROM THE MINES

EVERY MORNING MAMA GOT UP EARLY
SHE PUT ON HER BARGAIN BASEMENT SHOES
SHE SAID CHILDREN WILL YOU HURRY
IT'S A TWO MILE WALK TO SCHOOL

WE DIDN'T CARE IF WE LOOKED SILLY
IN SECOND HAND SHIRTS AND A SOUTHERN DRAWL
WHEN KIDS CALLED US HILLBILLY
IT DIDN'T BOTHER US AT ALL
WE WERE RICH AND WE KNEW IT
WE HAD LOVE WALL TO WALL

DADDY NEVER ACCEPTED LAME EXCUSES
THAT'S WHY WE ALL TOED THE LINE
MAMA DRESSED OUR CUTS AND BRUISES
WE LOTS OF LOVE AND HOMEMADE SHINE

THE PREACHER TOLD US EVERY SUNDAY
WE SHALL REAP THE SEEDS WE SOW
THAT'S WHY WE NEVER WENT HUNGRY
ALL THAT LOVE MADE OUR GARDEN GROW

WE DIDN'T CARE IF WE LOOKED SILLY
IN WORN OUT BOOTS AND COVERALLS

WHEN KIDS CALLED US HILLBILLY
THEY NEVER SEEN WHAT WE SAW
WE WERE RICH BUT NEVER SHOWED IT
LOVE'S THE GREATEST TREASURE OF ALL

WE WATCHED OUR NEIGHBORS IN A HURRY
THE POST OFFICE OPENED AT NINE
DADDY SAID MAMA DON'T YOU WORRY
WE DON'T BELONG IN THAT WELFARE LINE

MAMA NEVER SAID A SINGLE WORD
WE ALL KNEW HE WAS RIGHT
I GUESS HEAVEN MUST HAVE HEARD
MAMA READING THE BIBLE BY CANDLELIGHT

WAY DOWN LOW IN THE VALLEY
THERE STANDS A HOUSE AMONG THE PINES
WHERE CHILDREN WASH THEIR DIRTY FACES
WITH WATER CLEAR AS COLD MOONSHINE

MY WIFE MARY GETS UP EARLY
SHE PUTS ON HER BRAND NEW SHOES
SHE SAYS CHILDREN WILL YOU HURRY
PLEASE DON'T MISS THE BUS TO SCHOOL

THEY DON'T CARE IF THEY LOOK SILLY
IN BRAND NEW BOOTS AND COVERALLS
WHEN KIDS CALL THEM HILLBILLY
HAND IN HAND THEY STAND TALL
THEY ARE RICH AND THEY KNOW IT

LOVE'S THE GREATEST TREASURE OF ALL
YEAH THEY'RE RICH AND THEY KNOW IT
LOVE'S THE GREATEST TREASURE OF ALL

NOTE# A COUNTRY SONG ABOUT GROWING UP IN WILD
WONDERFUL WEST VIRGINIA

60

LOVE COMES IN MANY COLORS

IF I SAY I LOVE YOU
THERE'S NO NEED TO THINK I LIE
WHEN I SAY I'M THINKING OF YOU
IT'S BECAUSE I KNOW THE REASON WHY

I'M GIVING YOU ALL MY TOMORROWS
WITH EVERY DREAM THAT MIGHT COME TRUE
BECAUSE IN MY HEART I FEEL NO SORROW
WHEN EVER I SLEEP NEXT TO YOU

LOVE COMES IN MANY COLORS
JUST LIKE RAINBOWS AND WATERFALLS
THERE'S A THOUSAND WAYS TO SAY I LOVE YOU
IF ONLY I COULD SAY THEM ALL
LOVE COMES IN MANY COLORS
JUST LIKE A PAINTING ON THE WALL

BLUE SKIES SHINING IN YOUR EYES
I DON'T SEE A CLOUD IN SIGHT
WITH A HEART AS GOLD AS THE SUNRISE
YOU GUIDE ME THROUGH THE NIGHT

WHEN YOU SAY THAT YOU LOVE ME
I SEE THAT OLD MOON GLOW
WHEN YOU HANG SILVER STARS ABOVE ME
I SEE THAT YOU ALREADY KNOW

LOVE COMES IN MANY COLORS
JUST LIKE RAINBOWS AND WATERFALLS

THERE'S A THOUSAND WAYS TO SAY I LOVE YOU
IF ONLY I COULD SAY THEM ALL
LOVE COMES IN MANY COLORS
JUST LIKE A PAINTING ON THE WALL

I'M THROWING AWAY MY YESTERDAYS
WITH EVERY DREAM THAT NEVER CAME TRUE
BECAUSE ALL I SAW WERE SHADES OF GREY
UNTIL YOUR LOVE CAME SHINING THROUGH

WHEN THAT SONGBIRD SITS ON YOUR SHOULDER
AND THAT SMILE LIGHTS UP YOUR FACE
I AM YOUNG AGAIN INSTEAD OF OLDER
BECAUSE IN YOUR ARMS I FOUND A PLACE

WHERE LOVE COMES IN MANY COLORS
JUST LIKE RAINBOWS AND WATERFALLS
THERE'S A THOUSAND WAYS TO SAY I LOVE YOU
IF ONLY I COULD SAY THEM ALL
LOVE COMES IN MANY COLORS
LOVE COMES IN MANY COLORS
JUST LIKE A PAINTING ON THE WALL

NOTE# CLASSIC COUNTRY LOVE SONG

61

SHE'S GONE FISHING

HEY HEY I WENT FISHING THE OTHER DAY
AND I STAYED OUT ALL NIGHT
CAME HOME TO A HOUSE FULL OF ANGER
A PYRANNA READY TO STRIKE

SHE SAID I HOPE YOU CAUGHT THE BIG ONE
I HOPE YOU REELED HER IN
I'M LEAVING HOME TO FISH ON MY OWN
BABY I KNOW WHERE YOU BEEN

IT WASN'T DOWN AT THE RIVER
IT WASN'T DOWN AT THE LAKE
YOU TOOK YOUR POLE TO A NEW FISHING HOLE
YOU WERE FISHING FOR A HEARTACHE
UMM SHE'S GONE FISHING

I THOUGHT I HAD HER HOOKED
DANGLING FROM ALL MY LIES
SHE SAID DINNER AINT COOKED
BUT YOU CAN EAT YOUR ALIBIES

NOW SHE'S GONE FISHING AND I'M WISHING
HOME IS WHERE I SHOULD HAVE STAYED
LET ME BUY YOU A DRINK AND TELL YOU A STORY
ABOUT THE ONE THAT GOT AWAY

SHE SAID I HOPE YOU CAUGHT THE BIG ONE
I HOPE YOU REELED HER IN
I'M LEAVING HOME TO FISH ON MY OWN
BABY I KNOW WHERE YOU BEEN

IT WASN'T DOWN AT THE RIVER
IT WASN'T DOWN AT THE LAKE
YOU TOOK YOUR POLE TO A NEW FISHING HOLE
YOU WERE FISHING FOR A HEARTACHE
OH YEAH SHE'S GONE FISHING
HERE I SIT CALLING IT QUITS
I'VE LEARNED MY LESSON WELL
DON'T TAKE YOUR BUDDIES ON A TRIP
THEY LOVE TO FISH AND TELL

IT'S TOO LATE TO FISH OR CUT BAIT
I'M DIEING ON THE DOCK OF THE BAY
WITH NO HOPE OF SEEING HER BOBBERS FLOAT
WATCHING HER TACKLEBOX SWIM AWAY

SHE SAID I HOPE YOU CAUGHT THE BIG ONE
I HOPE YOU REELED HER IN
I'M LEAVING HOME TO FISH ON MY OWN
BABY I KNOW WHERE YOU BEEN

IT WASN'T DOWN AT THE RIVER
IT WASN'T DOWN AT THE LAKE
YOU TOOK YOUR POLE TO A NEW FISHING HOLE
YOU WERE FISHING FOR A HEARTACHE
OH YEAH.....AW SHE'S GONE FISHING

NOTE# THE ONE THAT GOT AWAY FROM ME/KIND OF SILLY
COUNTRY TUNE

62

TEARS IN THE WIND

WOMAN I WONDER WHERE YOU ARE NOW
DID YOU ESCAPE YOUR DESTINY
OR HAS FATE FOUND YOU OUT SOMEHOW
LIVING ON DREAMS AND MEMORIES

THERE ARE DARK CLOUDS IN MY EYES
AND THUNDER IN MY HEART
AN ACHE IN MY SOUL I CAN'T CONTROL
HOLDING ON IS THE HARDEST PART

HONEY CAN'T YOU HEAR ME CALLING
HERE COMES THOSE MEMORIES AGAIN
IT'S NOT RAIN THAT YOU SEE FALLING
IT'S ONLY MY TEARS IN THE WIND
TEARS IN THE WIND
THEY ARE ONLY LONELY
TEARS IN THE WIND

NOW CENTRAL CITY DOESN'T LOOK SO PRETTY
YOU LEFT ME CRYING BY THE TRACKS
YOUR BEDROOM LIGHT DOESN'T SHINE AT NIGHT
A SURE SIGN YOU AINT COMING BACK

NOW THE RIVERS ARE ALL OVERFLOWING
DON'T GET CAUGHT OUT ON THE ROAD
MY LOVE IS A STORM THAT KEEPS ON GROWING
I DON'T KNOW WHY IT DON'T EXPLODE

HONEY CAN'T YOU HEAR ME CALLING
HERE COMES THOSE MEMORIES AGAIN
IT'S NOT RAIN THAT YOU SEE FALLING
IT'S ONLY MY TEARS IN THE WIND TEARS IN THE WIND THEY ARE
ONLY LONELY TEARS IN THE WIND

NOW ALL THE BRIDGES ARE SINKING I'M
WISHING YOU WERE HERE
WITH ME I'M STRANDED ON THIS ISLAND THINKING IN LOVE
AINT NO PLACE TO BE

I PROMISED TO LOVE YOU FOREVER
I HAVE KEPT MY PROMISE IN VAIN
THERE'S NOT MUCH LEFT IN THIS OLD HEART
MY LOVE IS ALL THAT REMAINS

HONEY CAN'T YOU HEAR ME CALLING
HERE COMES THOSE MEMORIES AGAIN
IT'S NOT RAIN THAT YOU SEE FALLING
IT'S ONLY MY TEARS IN THE WIND
TEARS IN THE WIND
THEY ARE ONLY LONELY TEARS IN THE WIND THEY ARE ONLY
LONELY TEARS IN THE WIND

NOTE# REMEMBERING LOST LOVE IN A TRADITIONAL COUNTRY
TEAR JERKER

63

MAMA'S EYES

I'VE BEEN DOWN THIS ROAD TOO LONG
FEELING TIRED-FEELING ALONE
I FINALLY FOUND THE RIGHT WORDS
TO MY SONG I'M SINGING MY WAY BACK HOME

TAKE ME HOME OLD LONESOME HIGHWAY
TAKE ME BACK TO THOSE BLUE SKIES
CAUSE NO MATTER WHAT I DO OR WHAT I SAY
I CAN ALWAYS FIND LOVE IN MAMA'S EYES
MAMA'S EYES
CAN ALWAYS FIND LOVE IN MAMA'S EYES

NOW I'VE GOT MY DIRTY RAGS PACKED IN MY OLD SUITCASEI
OT MY THUMB STUCK IN THE AIR
I CAN'T WAIT TO SEE HER SMILING FACE
CAUSE I KNOW SHE'S WAITING THERE

KNOWING EVERY MAN MAKES HIS SHARE OF MISTAKES
DREAMS DON'T ALWAYS COME TRUE
NOW I'VE HAD MY SHARE OF HARD TIMES AND HEARTACHES
MAMA I'M COMING HOME TO YOU

TAKE ME HOME OLD LONESOME HIGHWAY
TAKE ME BACK TO THOSE BLUE SKIES
CAUSE NO MATTER WHERE I'VE BEEN OR THE SHAPE I'M IN
ICAN ALWAYS FIND LOVE IN MAMA'S EYES
MAMA'S EYES I CAN ALWAYS FIND LOVE IN MAMA'S EYES

FROM MISSISSIPPI TO THE MOUNTAINS OF WEST VIRGINIA
MY FOOTSTEPS FALL BACK IN LINE
MAMA SAID SON I KNOW YOU GOT IT IN YA
COME BACK AND SPEND SOME TIME
TAKE ME HOME OLD LONESOME HIGHWAY
TAKE ME BACK TO THOSE BLUE SKIES
CAUSE NO MATTER WHAT I'VE DONE OR THE MAN I'VE BECOME
CAN ALWAYS FIND LOVE IN MAMA'

EYES MAMA'S EYES I CAN ALWAYS FIND LOVE IN MAMA'S EYES I
CAN ALWAYS FIND LOVE IN MAMA'S EYES

NOTE# TRADITIONAL COUNTRY TRIBUTE TO MY MOTHER/GOD
REST HER SOUL

64

MACHO WOMAN

I MET HER IN A COLD DARK ALLEY
ALL ALONE BEHIND BILLY'S BAR
SHE SAID MY NAME IS SEXY SALLY
I SAID I KNOW WHO YOU ARE

IN HER LEATHER CLOTHES AND RINGS IN HER NOSE
SHE KICKED ME IN MY KNEE
WHILE SPITTING OUT PIECES OF HER BIG TOE
I HUMBLY HAD TO AGREE

YOU'RE A MACHO WOMAN
YOU DRINK BEER FROM A CAN
YOU WANT SOMEONE TO LOVE YOU
BUT I DON'T THINK I CAN
YOU'RE A MACHO WOMAN
YOU SHOULD HAVE BEEN A MAN

I SHOULDN'T HAVE SAID HER NECK WAS RED
AND I HATED HER HAIR
I'D BE DEAD IF SHE SCRATCHED MY HEAD
WITH CLAWS LIKE A GRIZZLY BEAR

YOU'RE A MACHO WOMAN
YOU DRINK BEER FROM A CAN
YOU WANT SOMEONE TO LOVE YOU
BUT I DON'T THINK I CAN
YOU'RE A MACHO WOMAN
YOU SHOULD HAVE BEEN A MAN

WELL SHE THREW ME DOWN ON THE GROUND
LAUGHED AND CALLED ME A WIMP
All THE DOCTORS SAY I'll BE OKAY
BUT I'LL ALWAYS HAVE A LIMP

YES SHE BLACKS MY EYES AND BUSTS MY LIPS
EVERY TIME SHE COMES MY WAY
BECAUSE HER NAME IS TATOOED ON MY HIPS
BELOW THE WORDS THAT SAY
YOU'RE A MACHO WOMAN
YOU DRINK BEER FROM A CAN
YOU WANT SOMEONE TO LOVE YOU
BUT I DON'T THINK I CAN
YOU'RE A MACHO WOMAN
YOU SHOULD HAVE BEEN A MAN
OH YOU'RE A MACHO WOMAN
YOU SHOULD HAVE BEEN A MAN

NOTE# YOU MEET STRANGE WOMEN IN BARS SO BEWARE/IT
COULD HAPPEN

65

DEVIL IN THE DARK

THE RAIN FALLS OUTSIDE MY WINDOW
I CAN HEAR IT HIT THE GROUND
MIDNIGHT COMES AND MIDNIGHT GOES
MY WORLD IS SPINNING UPSIDE DOWN

I SEE YOUR EYES BLAZING WITH DESIRE
IT'S A LOOK I KNOW SO WELL
I FEEL MY TEMPATURE IS GETTING HIGHER
I'M BURNING UP IN THIS FAIRYTALE

TONIGHT MY EMOTIONS ARE BOILING OVER
THE OCEAN IS FULL OF SHARKS
I FELL IN LOVE WITHOUT KNOWING
THERE ARE FLAMES INSIDE YOUR HEART
NOW I SEE YOUR FACE A GLOWING
YOU'RE A DEVIL IN THE DARK
YES YOU ARE A DEVIL IN THE DARK

WHEN THE NIGHTMARES COME WITHOUT CALLING
YOUR LOVE WON'T LET THEM STAY
WHEN THE SHADOWS ARE LONG AND FALLING
YOUR KISSES BLOW THEM ALL AWAY

NOW YOU'RE STEALING ALL MY PILLOWS
KICKING MY SHEETS TO THE FLOOR
YOU'RE KEEPING SECRETS THAT YOU KNOW
ONLY MAKES ME LOVE YOU MORE

TONIGHT THERE'S A HOT WIND BLOWING

AND SOMEWHERE A MAD DOG BARKS

FELL IN LOVE WITHOUT KNOWING

THERE ARE FLAMES INSIDE YOUR HEART

NOW YOUR TRUE COLORS ARE SHOWING

YOU'RE A DEVIL IN THE DARK

YES YOU ARE A DEVIL IN THE DARK

THE DAYLIGHT WILL FIND ME SLEEPING

WITH DREAMS OF YOU INSIDE MY HEAD

THE NIGHT TIME WILL FIND YOU CREEPING

AND CRAWLING BACK INTO MY BED

THAT'S WHEN THE TEMPATURE STARTS GETTING HIGHER

IN THIS ROOM FULL OF MAGIC SPELLS

YOU'RE THE SPARK THAT LIGHTS MY FIRE

I'M BURNING UP IN THIS FAIRYTALE

TONIGHT MY EMOTIONS ARE BOILING OVER

THE OCEAN IS FULL OF SHARKS

I FELL IN LOVE WITHOUT KNOWING

THERE ARE FLAMES INSIDE YOUR HEART

NOW I SEE YOUR FACE A GLOWING

YOU'RE A DEVIL IN THE DARK

OH I SEE YOUR FACE A GLOWING

OH YES YOU ARE A DEVIL IN THE DARK

DEVIL IN THE DARK

NOTE# YOU CAN'T IGNORE WHAT GOES ON BEHIND CLOSED DOORS MACHO WOMAN NOW IS YOURS/IN A COUNTRY TUNE FOREVER MORE

66

FAT'S IN THE FIRE

HONEY HONEY I DON'T WANT YOUR MONEY
I'VE GOT A TASTE FOR SOMETHING SWEET
HONEY HONEY IT MAY SOUND FUNNY
OU'RE LOOKING GOOD ENOUGH TO EAT

GIRL YOU GOT MY LITTLE WORLD TURNING
SPINNING OUT OF SIGHT
BABY YOU GOT MY LITTLE HEART BURNING
THE FAT'S IN THE FIRE TONIGHT
OH YEAH BABY I DON'T MEAN MAYBE
THE FAT'S IN THE FIRE TONIGHT

ONE LOOK AND MY BACON WAS COOKED
MY TASTE BUDS BOUNCED OFF MY PLATE
ONE TOUCH AND MY HAMBONE WAS HOOKED
RED HOT KISSES MELTING DOWN MY FACE

I LOVE YOU TODAY MORE THAN YESTERDAY
AND WHEN EVER MY PANTS GO TO ITCHIN
YOU COME ALONG WITH YOUR BUG SPRAY
ZAPPING THE FLY IN YOUR KITCHEN

BABY YOU GOT MY LITTLE DOG DROOLING
FRENCH FRIED FEELINGS IN THE FIRELIGHT
BABY MY MEATBALLS AINT FOOLING
THE FAT'S IN THE FIRE TONIGHT
OH YEAH BABY I DON'T MEAN MAYBE
THE FAT'S IN THE FIRE TONIGHT

SO STIR THAT POT WITH LOVE ALOT
WHIP UP YOUR SECRET RECIPE
I NEED YOUR BODY SMOKING HOT
TO FEED THE NEED IN ME

SO SIZZLE AND SHAKE AND MAKE NO MISTAKE
HONEY YOU'RE THE ONLY ONE
WHEN I'VE HAD MY FILL OF STEAK ON THE GRILL
TURN ME OVER BECAUSE I'M DONE
GIRL YOU GOT MY LITTLE WORLD TURNING
SPINNING OUT OF SIGHT
BABY YOU GOT MY LITTLE HEART BURNING
THE FAT'S IN THE FIRE TONIGHT
OH YEAH BABY I DON'T MEAN MAYBE
THE FAT'S IN THE FIRE TONIGHT
OH YEAH BABY I DON'T MEAN MAYBE
THE FAT'S IN THE FIRE TONIGHT

NOTE# KIND OF THINKING ABOUT HANK JR SONGS AND BBQ'S/
GO FIGURE/ COULD BE THE NEXT BIG HIT/HA-HA

67

POUND ME LIKE A NAIL

MY ANGEL I SEE YOU COMING
DRAGGING YOUR BAG OF
TOOLS DOES HEAVEN KNOW YOUR MISSING
WITH ALL THEIR GOLDEN RULES

YOUR STARS THEY FALL AND SHATTER
CRASHING DOWN ON MY FACE
I WATCH YOU CLIMB THE LADDER
AND YOU BOP INTO SPACE

YOU'RE THE HAMMER IN MY HEART HONEY
YOU GOT ME UNDER A SPELL
I'LL BEND BUT I WON'T BREAK BABY
SO POUND ME LIKE A NAIL
POUND ME POUND ME POUND ME
POUND ME LIKE A NAIL

DRIVE ME HARD THROUGH THE DARKNESS
HIT ME ON MY HEAD
SPLIT THE SEAMS OF ALL MY DREAMS
NAIL ME TO YOUR BED

CRUSH MY BONES LIKE ROLLING STONES
GIVE ME ALL YOU GOT
BITE THE BULLET AND HOLD THE PHONE
GIVE ME YOUR BEST SHOT

WITH LIPS THAT SAY THEY LOVE ME
WHEN MY HEART BEGINS TO SWELL
YOU'RE COMING DOWN FROM MILES ABOVE ME
SO POUND ME LIKE A NAIL POUND ME
POUND ME POUND ME POUND ME LIKE A NAIL

IT'S TOO LATE FOR HEAVEN'S SAKE
MY PIG'S ABOUT TO SQUEAL
LIKE EARTHQUAKES I TREMBLE AND SHAKE
UNTIL YOUR HOLE GETS FILLED

MY OCEAN ROLLS OUT OF CONTROL
DROWNING YOUR BODY IN SWEAT
THE WIND HOWLS LOOK AT ME NOW
MY NAIL IS SOAKING WET

YOU'RE THE HAMMER IN MY HEART HONEY
YOU GOT ME UNDER A SPELL
I'LL BEND BUT I WON'T BREAK BABY
SO POUND ME LIKE A NAIL
POUND ME POUND ME
POUND ME POUND ME LIKE A NAIL
OH POUND ME POUND ME POUND ME
POUND ME LIKE A NAIL

NOTE# LISTENING TO THE BEATLES' HELTER SKELTER WHEN I
WROTE THIS ONE

68

MY PIE

I'VE HEARD THOSE VOICES TALKING
RUMOURS UP AND DOWN THE LINE
THEY SAY YOU'VE BEEN WALKING
MESSING WITH THAT GIRL OF MINE

I'M HERE TO TELL YOU BOY
I'M GOING TO BLACK YOUR EYE
YOU BETTER HEED MY WARNING BOY
OR YOU JUST MIGHT DIE
SHE'S MY FAVORITE SLICE OF HEAVEN
SHE'S THE APPLE IN MY EYE
GET AWAY FROM MY JOY
GET AWAY FROM MY PIE

I'LL FILL YOU SO FULL OF HOLES
THE WIND WILL BLOW RIGHT THROUGH
YOU SAY THAT YOU LOVE HER
WELL I SAY I LOVE HER TOO

SO MOVE ALONG LITTLE DOGGIE
DRAG YOUR SORRY TAIL ON HOME
RUN AND CRY TO YOUR DADDY
CALL YOUR LAWYER ON THE PHONE

CAUSE I'M HERE TO TELL YOU BOY
I'M GOING TO BLACK YOUR EYE

BETTER HEED MY WARNING BOY
OR YOU JUST MIGHT DIE
SHE'S MY FAVORITE SLICE OF HEAVEN
SHE'S THE APPLE IN MY EYE
GET AWAY FROM MY JOY
GET AWAY FROM MY PIE

I GUESS I'LL HAVE TO SHOW YOU
JUST HOW MUCH IT HURTS
I GUESS I'LL HAVE TO KILL YOU
IF YOU STEAL MY DESSERT

YOU KNOW SHE'S MY LOVING WOMAN
SHE'S THE SWEETEST IN THE LAND
PEACHES AND CREAM AND STRAWBERRY DREAMS
THINGS ARE GETTING OUT OF HAND

SO I'M HERE TO TELL YOU BOY
I'M GOING TO BLACK YOUR EYE
BETTER HEED MY WARNING BOY
OR YOU JUST MIGHT DIE
SHE'S MY FAVORITE SLICE OF HEAVEN
SHE'S THE APPLE IN MY EYE
GET AWAY FROM MY JOY
GET AWAY FROM MY PIE
YEAH GET AWAY
OH OH GET AWAY FROM MY PIE
GET AWAY GET AWAY

NOTE# THINKING ABOUT A BOY NAMED SUE(JOHNNY CASH)
WHEN I WROTE THIS SONG MAYBE I WAS JUST HUNGRY/WHO
KNOWS

69

OH HALOWWEENIE

IT'S TWELVE 0 CLOCK ON SALEM'S LOT
THE DEVIL COMES TO GATHER SOULS
FROM THE DUNGEON OF DREAMS A VOICE SCREAMS
PLAY THAT ROCK AND ROLL

WE GOT FRANKENSTEIN HIDING IN THE BEDROOM
GIVING ALL THE GIRLS A FLING
WE GOT HIS BRIDE TWISTED AND TIED
SCREAMING I'LL BREAK HIS DING A LING

HERE COMES HOLLOWWEENIE IN HER STRING BIKINI
DANCING WITH ALL THE GUYS
OH HALLOWWEENIE THOSE ARE NOT SO TEENY
YOUR PUMPKINS AINT GOT ANY EYES
OH HALLOWWEENIE SHE'S NO DREAM OF GENIE
SHE'S A NIGHTMARE IN DISQUISE

WE GOT ELVIS AND HIS PELVIS
GLUED TO HIS BAR STOOL
WITCHES ON BROOMS FLY AROUND THE ROOM
SINGING DON'T BE MEAN AND CRUEL

WE GOT GHOULIES MESSING WITH THE STOOLIES
SPIDERS CRAWLING UP THE WALLS
WE GOT MICHAEL JORDEN AND LIZZIE BORDEN
PLAYING WITH HIS BALLS

HERE COMES HALLOWWEENIE IN HER STRING BIKINI
DANCING WITH ALL THE GUYS

OH HALLOWWEENIE THOSE ARE NOT SO TEENY
YOUR PUMPKINS AINT GOT ANY EYES
OH HALLOWWEENIE SHE'S NO DREAM OF GENIE
SHE'S A NIGHTMARE IN DISQUISE

WE GOT SKEIETONS IN THE CLOSET KISSING
WEREWOLVES KNOCKING ON THE DOOR
WE GOT DRACULA IN THE BATHROOM PISSING
EYEBALLS FLOATING ON THE FLOOR
WE GOT CATS AND CRAZY DING BATS
TIGER WOODS TEACHING GOLF
WE GOT FRED ACTING LIKE HE'S DEAD
WILMA KNOCKED HIS SOCKS OFF

HERE COMES HALLOWWEENIE WITHOUT HER STRING BIKINI
HER KNOTS HAVE COME UNTIED
OH HALLOWWEENIE SHE'S NO DREAM OF GENIE
AND MUCH TO MY SURPRISE
OH HALLOWWEENIE SHE REALLY WAS A WEENIE
SHE WAS JUST ANOTHER GUY
OH NOOH MY
OH HALLOWWEENIE OH HALLOWWEENIE
LET'S GET OUT OF HERE

NOTE# HALLOWEEN SONG/HOPE YOU ARE AMUSED

70

SEASONS OUT OF TIME

SUMMER DAYS HAVE PASSED AWAY
OLD MAN WINTER IS AT MY DOOR
WE HAD OUR FUN IN THAT SUMMER SUN
BUT IT DON'T SHINE ANYMORE

ALL BECAUSE OF YOU AND ME
OUR FOOTSTEPS FELL OUT OF LINE
ALL THE LOVE YOU HAD WENT FROM GOOD TO BAD
THIS IS ALL YOU LEFT BEHIND

SEASONS OUT OF TIME
I'M NOT YOURS AND YOU'RE NOT MINE
NOW I'M TRAPPED HERE FOREVER
REMEMBERING YOU IN THE SEASONS OUT OF TIME

THE BIRDS FLY NORTH FOR THE WINTER
T ALWAYS SNOWS IN MID JULY
A DECEMBER SPRING DOESN'T CHANGE A THING
THERE ARE DAYS I STILL CRY

IT'S ALL BECAUSE I LOVE YOU
OH GIRL I LOVE YOU SO
I REALLY TRIED TO KEEP YOU SATISFIED
I HELD ON BUT LET YOU GO

SEASONS OUT OF TIME
I'M NOT YOURS AND YOU'RE NOT MINE
NOW I'M TRAPPED HERE FOREVER
REMEMBERING YOU IN THE SEASONS OUT OF TIME

ON THE ROAD OUTSIDE OF TOWN
THE SIGN SAYS WELCOME TO MISERY
I'M IN NO DANGER FROM PASSING STRANGERS
BECAUSE EVERY STRANGER LOOKS LIKE ME

NOW I KNOW THAT IT'S ALL OVER
ROSES WON'T GROW ON THE VINE
ALL THE LOVE YOU HAD WENT FROM GOOD TO BAD
THIS IS ALL YOU LEFT BEHIND

SEASONS OUT OF TIME
I'M NOT YOURS AND YOU'RE NOT MINE
NOW I'M TRAPPED HERE FOREVER
REMEMBERING YOU IN THE SEASONS OUT OF TIME
OH YES I KNOW THESE SEASONS OUT OF TIME

NOTE# WHAT CAN I SAY/ANOTHER TEARJERKER/OH WOE IS ME/
HA-HA

71

I'M GOING HOME

WHEN LOVE COMES IN MANY COLORS
YOU CAN POUND ME LIKE A NAIL
SHE'S GONE FISHING WITH MACHO WOMAN
OH HALLOWWEENIE FOUND TRUE LOVE IN JAIL

SOMEONE SHOT THE DEVIL IN THE DARK
SHE WAS A ROCK HE COULDN'T ROLL
SHE'S GETTING RICH IN THE PARK
SELLING PIECES OF HIS HEART AND SOUL

I'M GOING HOME
STRAIGHT BACK TO MY MAMA'S EYES
TOMORROW I'LL BE GONE
TO A PLACE WHERE LOVE NEVER DIES
I'M GOING HOME
I'M GOING HOME

NOW MY FAT AINT IN THE FIRE
NO MORE TEARS IN THE WIND
I DON'T DRINK WITH FOOLS AND LIARS
I'M STRAIGHTER THAN I'VE EVER BEEN

I'M LEAVING BEHIND SEASONS OUT OF TIME
HEAVEN WAITS RIGHT OVER THE HILL
THIS HUNGER NEEDS A RAY OF SUNSHINE
MY PIE WAITS ON MAMA'S WINDOW SILL

I'M GOING HOME
AS FAST AS MY FEET WILL FLY
TOMORROW I'LL BE GONE
GOD WILLING AND THE CREEK DON'T RISE
I'M GOING HOME
I'M GOING HOME

THAT HILLBILLY SONG PLAYS ON
AND ON THROUGH THE SPEAKERS IN MY CAR
MY HEADLIGHTS SHINE INTO THE GREAT BEYOND
'M DRINKING COFFEE FROM A MASON JAR

MAMA SAYS AS SHE BAKES HER BREAD
'M GOING TO SEE MY SON AGAIN
DADDY SAYS AS HE SHAKES HIS HEAD
LOOK AT WHAT THE CAT DRAGGED IN

I MADE IT HOME
STRAIGHT BACK TO MY MAMA'S EYES
OW I'M NOT ALONE
IN A PLACE WHERE LOVE NEVER DIES
I MADE IT HOME
MADE IT HOME

NOTE# SONG TITLES FROM THE TRAVELLING HILLBILLY

72

LOGAN TOWN

HERE COMES MY SNAPPY PAPPY
DRESSED IN HIS BLUE SUEDE SUIT
HERE COMES MY WHAMMY MAMMY
KICKING HIGH IN HER ELVIS BOOTS

LITTLE SISTER DOES THE TWISTER
WHILE BIG SISTER SINGS THE BLUES
LITTLE BROTHER RUNS FOR COVER
SANDY IS JUMPING LIKE A KANGAROO

IT'S A HOE DOWN IN LOGAN TOWN
PLEASE COME DRESSED AS YOU ARE
EVERY NIGHT WHEN THE SUN GOES DOWN
WE BELLY UP TO THE BAR
SOON AFTER JUST A COUPLE OF ROUNDS
WE ALL LOOK LIKE SUPERSTARS
HERE WE ARE . . . . IN LOGAN TOWN

UNCLE GENE NEVER COMES CLEAN
WHEN HE TELLS A DIRTY JOKE
UNCLE SONNY LOVES HIS MONEY
AND BROWN TOBACCO IN A POKE

AUNT LINDA MAY LOOK SUSPENDED
WHEN SHE DOES THE BUGGALOO
AUNT BRENDA IS GETTING WINDED
SHE LOVES TO BOOGIE TOO

IT'S A SHOWDOWN IN LOGAN TOWN
BUY YOUR BULLETS AT THE BAR
EVERY NIGHT WHEN THE SUN GOES DOWN
WE GO SHOOTING AT THE STARS
SOON AFTER JUST A COUPLE OF ROUNDS
WE SHOW OFF OUR BULLET SCARS
HERE WE ARE . . . . IN LOGAN TOWN

HERE COMES PAT'S PINK CADILLAC
SHE'S LOOKING GOOD IN THAT FIFTYFIVE
THERE'S TRISH WITH TEDDY'S CATFISH
HER COOKING MAKES HIM COME ALIVE

THERE GOES MY HAPPY PAPPY
ROCKING IN HIS BLUE SUEDE SHOES
THERE GOES MY WHAMMY MAMMY
YOU KNOW SHE LOVED ELVIS TOO

IT'S A RUN DOWN IN LOGAN TOWN
PLACE YOUR BETS ON THE BAR
EVERY NIGHT WHEN THE SUN GOES DOWN
WE FLEX ALL OUR MUSCLE CARS
SOON AFTER JUST A COUPLE OF ROUNDS
WE WRECK OUR DREAMS AMONG THE STARS
HERE WE ARE . . . . IN LOGAN TOWN
SOON AFTER JUST A COUPLE OF ROUNDS
WE ALL LOOK LIKE SUPERSTARS
HERE WE ARE . . . . IN LOGAN TOWN
OH HERE WE ARE . . . . IN LOGAN TOWN

NOTE#COUNTRY TUNE *IONE* FOR THE FAMILY

73

I'LL STOP RIGHT HERE

THERE ARE SO MANY PARTS
AND PIECES YOU CAN'T SEE
LIVING HERE INSIDE MY HEART
A TREASURE TROVE OF MEMORIES

I ALMOST FORGOT TO STOP
BEFORE IT WAS TOO LATE
BIG SHOTS WITH THEIR CASH CROPS
THEY HAVE SEALED THEIR FATE

I COULD GO ON AND ON
BUT I'LL STOP RIGHT HERE
LITTLE BOY BLUE IN HIS KIDDIE POOL
LITTLE GIRL WITH HER MAKEUP SMEARED
TEENAGERS DRIVING OFF TO SCHOOL
LAUGHING WHEN THEY MISS A GEAR
I COULD GO ON
AND ON BUT I'LL STOP RIGHT HERE

IT'S NOT HARD TO REMEMBER
BACK TO DAYS OF OLD
IT ALWAYS FELT LIKE DECEMBER
BECAUSE MY SOUL WAS COLD

I ALMOST FORGOT THE SUNSHINE
BREAKING THROUGH AT DAWN
THANK GOD I STOPPED IN TIME
BEFORE THE LIGHT WAS GONE

I COULD GO ON AND ON
BUT I'LL STOP RIGHT HERE
LITTLE BOY BLUE IN HIS KIDDIE POOL
LITTLE GIRL WITH HER MAKEUP SMEARED
TEENAGERS DRIVING OFF TO SCHOOL
LAUGHING WHEN THEY MISS A GEAR
I COULD GO ON AND ON
BUT I'LL STOP RIGHT HERE

THERE ARE SO MANY PARTS
AND PIECES YOU CAN'T SEE
LIVING HERE INSIDE MY HEART
A TRESURE TROVE OF MEMORIES

I ALMOST FORGOT TO STOP
BEFORE LOVE TURNED INTO HATE
BIG SHOTS WITH THEIR CASH CROPS
DEADLINES HAVE SEALED THEIR FATE

I COULD GO ON AND ON
BUT I'LL STOP RIGHT HERE
LITTLE BOY BLUE IN HIS KIDDIE POOL
LITTLE GIRL WITH HER MAKEUP SMEARED
TEENAGERS DRIVING OFF TO SCHOOL
LAUGHING WHEN THEY MISS A GEAR
I COULD GO ON AND ON
BUT I'LL STOP RIGHT HERE

NOTE#WHAT'S MORE IMPORTANT MONEY OR FAMILY?/LISTENING
TO DON MCLEAN'S AMERICAN PIE AND VINCENT WHEN I WROTE
THIS ONE

74

FOR YOU AND ME

GO AHEAD AND SUE ME
IF THAT'S WHAT YOU NEED TO DO
AND WHEN YOU'RE THROUGH WITH ME
I'LL WRITE ANOTHER SONG FOR YOU

NOBODY KNOWS ME BETTER
THAN EACH AND EVERYONE OF YOU
DIG OUT THOSE OLD LOVE LETTERS
GOD KNOWS I WROTE A FEW

I'M THE ONE WHO HAS NOTHING
BUT A POCKETFUL OF MEMORIES
I STILL TREASURE EVERY MOMENT
AND THE DREAMS YOU COULDN'T SEE
FOR EVERY LOVER WHO DISCOVERED
JUST HOW CRAZY LOVE CAN BE
THIS ONE'S FOR YOU AND ME

THERE WERE DAYS I COULDN'T SAVE
A SINGLE SECOND OF TIME
I WAS BUSY TRYING TO MISBEHAVE
AND COMMIT THE PERFECT CRIME

JUST BY STEALING YOUR LOVE AWAY
I MADE YOUR KISSES MINE
JUST BY MURDERING ALL MY YESTERDAYS
YOU LEFT MY HEART BEHIND

I'M THE ONE WHO HAS NOTHING
BUT A POCKETFUL OF MEMORIES
I STILL TREASURE EVERY MOMENT
AND THE DREAMS YOU COULDN'T SEE
FOR EVERY LOVER WHO DISCOVERED
JUST HOW CRAZY LOVE CAN BE
THIS ONE'S FOR YOU AND ME
WHEN I END UP IN COURT
AND HEAVEN HEARS MY PLEA
CUPID SAYS I MUST REPORT
I'M GUILTY AS CAN BE

FOR HOLDING BACK THE LAST SONG
ON A COOL SUMMER BREEZE
FROM THE PAST THE FUTURE MARCHES ON
THROUGH A FOOL'S WINTER FREEZE

I'M THE ONE WHO HAS NOTHING
BUT A POCKETFUL OF MEMORIES
I STILL TREASURE EVERY MOMENT
AND THE DREAMS YOU COULDN'T SEE
FOR EVERY LOVER WHO DISCOVERED
JUST HOW CRAZY LOVE CAN BE
THIS ONE'S FOR YOU AND ME

NOTE# SOFT ROCK/POP

75

I WAS ONLY HAVING FUN

I STAYED AT THE HOTEL CALIFORNIA
BEYOND THE YELLOW BRICK ROAD
I USE TO SWIM AGAINST THE WIND
AND LET MY AQUALUNG EXPLODE

YOU JUST HAD TO BE THERE
WHERE THE STAIRWAY TO HEAVEN BEGINS
YOU ARE WELCOME TO MY NIGHTMARE
LET'S GET BACK IN BLACK AGAIN

I DROVE MY PARENTS CRAZY
BUT I WAS ONLY HAVING FUN
MAMA DIDN'T LIKE THE BEATLES
DADDY DIDN'T LIKE NEIL YOUNG
THEY LOVED WAYLON AND WILLIE
AND EVERY SONG CONWAY SUNG

I KNEW TAKING L.S.D. WAS RISKY
BEWARE OF POT THAT SMELLED LIKE PINE
I GOT DRUNK ON ROT GUT WHISKEY
AND HIGH ON STRAWBERRY WINE

PINK FLOYD TOOK ME INTO THE VOID
BEYOND THE DARK SIDE OF THE MOON
ON THE SABBATH I GOT SO PARANOID
AFRAID THE TRIP WOULD END TOO SOON

I DROVE MY PARENTS CRAZY
BUT I WAS ONLY HAVING FUN

MAMA DIDN'T LIKE THE BEATLES
DADDY DIDN'T LIKE NEIL YOUNG
THEY LOVED HANK AND JOHNNY
AND EVERY SONG LORETTA SUNG

I RODE THE YELLOW SUBMARINE
WITH LUCY IN THE SKY
I SAT NEXT TO DON MCLEAN
PIGGING OUT ON AMERICAN PIE

FOR THOSE THAT WERE THERE
YOU KNOW HOW THE STORY ENDS
FREEBIRD FLEW THROUGH THE AIR
DISAPPEARED LIKE DUST IN THE WIND

MY PARENTS ARE DRIVING ME CRAZY
IN THE HOUSE OF THE RISING SUN
DADDY DOESN'T LIKE THE BEATLES
MAMA DOESN'T LIKE NEIL YOUNG
THEY LOVE THE RIGHTEOUS BROTHERS
AND EVERY SONG ELVIS SUNG
MY YOUTH MUST ADMIT THE TRUTH
I WAS ONLY HAVING FUN

NOTE# TRIBUTE TO SOME OF MY FAVORITE SONGS AND ARTISTS
AND MY PARENTS TOO

76

I DREAMED I WAS ONE

I COULD GO ON AND ON
ABOUT DAYS OF FUTURE PASSED
WISH I HAD WROTE THAT SONG
SO MY MOOD WOULD LAST

IN MY JOURNEY TO INFINITY
I FOUND NOTHING LEFT TO LOSE
SOMEONE THREW AWAY THE KEY
TO THESE FOLSOM PRISON BLUES

THE HITS THAT DROVE ME CRAZY
WHEN I WAS VERY YOUNG
DADDY CALLED ME LAZY
MAMA CALLED ME SON
LISTENING TO THE LEGACY OF LEGENDS
I DREAMED THAT I WAS ONE

SO MANY SONGS THAT MOVED ME
AND TOOK MY BREATH AWAY
A COLLECTION OF MEMORIES AND MADNESS
FROM MY WILD AND WOOLY DAYS

RUMOURS OF LOVE AND FLEETWOOD CADILLACS
STABBED MY HEART WITH SPEARS
BAD COMPANY FOLLOWED ME DOWN THE TRACKS
AND HELPED ME DRINK MY BEER

THE HITS THAT DROVE ME CRAZY
WHEN I WAS VERY YOUNG

DADDY CALLED ME LAZY

MAMA CALLED ME SON

I PRETENDED I WAS A LEGEND

AND MY SONGS WERE NUMBER ONE

YOU AND ME AND BOBBY MCGEE

PLAYING GAMES IN THE DARK

RUNNING AROUND LIKE WE WERE FREE

LOOKING FOR A PLACE TO PARK

THOSE DAYS OF OLD ARE SOLID GOLD

BUT IF YOU CAN'T DECIDE

WHERE EVER THE MUSIC IS SOLD

BUY A TICKET TO RIDE

THE HITS THAT DROVE ME CRAZY

WHEN I WAS VERY YOUNG

DADDY CALLED ME LAZY

MAMA CALLED ME SON

LISTENING TO THE LEGACY OF LEGENDS

I DREAMED THAT I WAS ONE

NOTE# SOFT ROCK/POP-SPIN OFF OF I WAS ONLY HAVING FUN

77

SPOONS

LET ME TELL YOU A TALE
HOW SHE COMMITTED THE PERFECT CRIME
THE DAY SHE RUNG MY BELL
I THOUGHT IT WAS DINNER TIME

WHEN I BEGGED FOR A TASTE
SHE SPRAYED MY LIPS WITH MACE
AND HANDED ME A SPOON
WHEN SHE SLAPPED MY HAPPY FACE
MY TEETH FLEW INTO OUTER SPACE
AND LANDED ON THE MOON

OH WHAT A SIGHT THAT NIGHT
DOWN ON MY KNEES TO PURPOSE
WITH HER FIST CLENCHED UP TIGHT
SHE SMILED AND BROKE MY NOSE

I KNEW THEN I COULDN'T WIN
SO I SURRENDERED UP MY HEART
SHE GRABBED MY LITTLE WHITE FLAG
AND BURNED IT IN THE DARK

WHEN I BEGGED FOR A TASTE
SHE SPRAYED MY LIPS WITH MACE
AND HANDED ME A SPOON
WHEN SHE SLAPPED MY HAPPY FACE
MY TEETH FLEW INTO OUTER SPACE
AND LANDED ON THE MOON

WHAT IS LOVE BUT A DRUG
WHEN YOU STICK THE NEEDLE IN
I WAS DIEING FOR A HUG
WHEN SHE CRAWLED INSIDE MY SKIN

LET ME TELL YOU A TALE
WHEN SHE COMMITS THE PERFECT CRIME
THE DAY SHE RINGS YOUR BELL
IT'S NOT REALLY DINNER TIME

WHEN YOU ASK FOR A TASTE
SHE SPRAYS YOUR LIPS WITH MACE
AND HANDS YOU A SPOON
WHEN SHE SLAPS YOUR HAPPY FACE
YOUR GUMS FLAP IN OUTER SPACE
AND LAND ON THE MOON
WHEN YOUR HUNGER BECOMES YOUR FATE
SHE'S ALL OUT OF SPOONS

NOTE# FEELING GOOD AND FEELING BAD ABOUT ALL THE LOVE
AND DRUGS I HAD SOMETIMES IT'S A FINE LINE BETWEEN THE
TWO

78

STRONG ENOUGH TO CARRY ON

LET ME EXPLAIN THE LOVE AND PAIN
AND WHERE MY THOUGHTS OCCUR
SOMEWHERE DEEP INSIDE MY BRAIN
YOU CAN TALK TO HER

LET ME EXPLAIN THE HOT SUMMER RAIN
YOU KNOW SOMETIMES IT POURS
FALLING DOWN ON THAT OLD COAL TRAIN
MEMORIES ROLLING PAST HER DOOR

SHE WILL ANSWER ALL YOUR QUESTIONS
LONG AFTER I AM GONE
SHE KNOWS ME BETTER THAN MYSELF
SHE'S STRONG ENOUGH TO CARRY ON
SHE KNOWS ME LIKE NO ONE ELSE
SHE'S STRONG ENOUGH TO CARRY ON

I CAN'T EXPLAIN HOW LIFE HAS CHANGED
AND WHEN FRIENDSHIP FIRST OCCURRED
I GUESS MY LIFE WAS PREORDAINED
TO ALWAYS BE FRIENDS WITH HER

NO LONGER THE LOVER THAT COMPLAINS
AFTER ALL THE CRAZY YEARS
A STRONGER LOVE BROKE THE CHAINS
AND LEFT ME HAPPY HERE

SHE WILL ANSWER ALL YOUR QUESTIONS
LONG AFTER I AM GONE

SHE KNOWS ME BETTER THAN MYSELF
SHE'S STRONG ENOUGH TO CARRY ON
SHE KNOWS ME LIKE NO ONE ELSE
SHE'S STRONG ENOUGH TO CARRY ON

LET ME EXPLAIN THE LOVE AND PAIN
AND WHERE MY THOUGHTS OCCUR
SOMEWHERE DEEP INSIDE MY BRAIN
A SPECIAL PLACE FOR HER
LET ME EXPLAIN THE COLD WINTER RAIN
YOU KNOW SOMETIMES IT POURS
FALLING DOWN ON THAT OLD COAL TRAIN
MEMORIES ROLLING PAST HER DOOR

SHE WILL ANSWER ALL YOUR QUESTIONS
LONG AFTER I AM GONE
SHE KNOWS ME BETTER THAN MYSELF
SHE'S STRONG ENOUGH TO CARRY ON
SHE KNOWS ME LIKE NO ONE ELSE
SHE'S STRONG ENOUGH TO CARRY ON

NOTE# FOR THE ONES THAT KNOW ME AND KNOW WHO THIS
IS FOR THE MOTHER OF MY SON AND SO MUCH MORE/COUNTRY
TO THE MAX

79

BALLS OF STEEL

FOR ALL THE GUYS OUT THERE
BEWARE OF LOVE'S SWEET TENDER TRAP
BECAUSE IF YOU TOUCH THEM ANYWHERE
YOUR NOSEY FACE MIGHT GET SLAPPED

IF YOU SAY WORDS THE WRONG WAY
YOU MIGHT END UP ON REPORT
BECAUSE LADIES HAVE BALLS OF STEEL TODAY
THEY MIGHT ROLL YOU INTO COURT

WHAT CAN THE REAL ROMANTICS DO
SO AFRAID TO JOKE AND CARRY ON
BECAUSE REAL INTENTIONS MIGHT GET SUED
AND EVERYTHING YOU OWN IS GONE

SOME OF US SEPARATE LOVE FROM LUST
WHILE OTHERS PURSUE THEIR PASSION DIFFERANTLY
IT'S GETTING HARDER TO EARN WOMEN'S TRUST
BECAUSE OF THOSE WITH CAVEMAN MENTALITY

YOU CAN LOOK BUT YOU CAN'T TOUCH
NOT UNTIL THEIR LIPS SAY OKAY
BECAUSE LOVE AND HAPPINESS MEANS TOO MUCH
TO LET FOOLS GET IN THE WAY

ON THE LAW SHE WILL NOT BUDGE
OR CHANGE HER POINT OF VIEW
THE LADY JUDGE MIGHT HOLD A GRUDGE
AND THROW THE BOOK AT YOU

JUST FOR SOMETHING YOU MIGHT HAVE SAID
OR SOMETHING YOU MIGHT HAVE DONE
BETTER KEEP THOSE THOUGHTS INSIDE YOUR HEAD
AND DON'T LET YOUR FINGERS RUN

IF YOU SAY WORDS THE WRONG WAY
YOU MIGHT END UP ON REPORT
BECAUSE LADIES HAVE BALLS OF STEEL TODAY
THEY MIGHT ROLL YOU INTO COURT

80

THE END

NOW MY FRIENDS I'VE REACHED THE END
I'M GLAD YOU CAME ALONG
WHAT A STRANGE TRIP IT'S BEEN
TRAVELING THROUGH POETRY AND SONG

NOW IT'S TIME TO FREE MY MIND
STUCK BETWEEN RIGHT AND WRONG
IT'S A CRIME TO BE LEFT BEHIND
ON THE ROAD TOO LONG

NOW THE JOURNEY OF A MILLION MILES
IT MUST STOP RIGHT HERE
BEFORE I GET TRAPPED BY THE SMILES
THE LAUGHTER AND THE TEARS

NOW ALL MY MEMORIES ARE NEATLY FRAMED
RIGHT HERE INSIDE THIS BOOK
I CAN ONLY FIND MYSELF TO BLAME
FOR THE PATH I TOOK

THINK OF MUSIC THAT HIDES BEHIND
EVERY WORD THAT I'M SAYING
THINK OF SONGS INSIDE YOUR MIND
LIKE A BROKEN RECORD PLAYING

WHEN MY THOUGHTS ARE SUDDENLY CAUGHT
WITH MY SORROW ON DISPLAY
THE ONLY LESSON I'VE BEEN TAUGHT
THE PAST IS TOMORROW'S YESTERDAY

THERE'S NO GETTING OFF THE HOOK
WHEN LOVE QUESTIONS MY DESIRE
THE ANSWERS LIE INSIDE THIS BOOK
FOR CURIOUS EYES TO ADMIRE
SWINGING ON THE ROPE OF HOPE
THROUGH THE JUNGLE OF DISMAY
LOOKING FOR A REASON TO COPE
WITH REJECTION ALONG THE WAY

I SIT AND CURSE THE UNIVERSE
WITH MY PEN IN HAND
I QUIT WHEN THE STARS BURST
AND CRAP HITS THE FAN
WRITING SONGS AND POETRY IN VERSE
BARELY ESCAPING THE GARBAGE CAN

ONLY TO DIE BETWEEN THE COVERS
UNTIL THEY ARE RESURRECTED
LIKE ARROWS THROUGH THE HEART OF LOVERS
ALWAYS EXPECT THE UNEXPECTED